How to Unblock Everything on the Internet

Other books by Ankit Fadia

Want to learn more about ethical hacking? Want to increase your knowledge in various Ethical Hacking topics? Want to complete your collection of books on Ethical Hacking by internationally bestselling author Ankit Fadia? Other books authored by Ankit Fadia that you will enjoy reading:

- ✓ **E-mail Hacking**
- ✓ **Windows Hacking** (New, 2nd edition)
- ✓ **Intrusion Alert** (Co-Authored by *Manu Zacharia*)
- ✓ **System Forensics** (Co-Authored by *Boonlia Prince Komal)*
- ✓ **Software Hacking** (Co-Authored by *Nishant Das Patnaik*)
- ✓ **Encryption: Protecting Your Data** (Co-Authored by *Jaya Bhattacharjee*)

Rush to your nearest bookstore or visit www.ankitfadia.in to buy these books and complete your collection today.

How to Unblock Everything on the Internet

Second Edition

Ankit Fadia

VIKAS®

VIKAS® PUBLISHING HOUSE PVT LTD

VIKAS® PUBLISHING HOUSE PVT LTD

E-28, Sector-8, **Noida**-201301 (UP) India

Phone: +91-120-4078900 • Fax: +91-120-4078999

Registered Office: 576, Masjid Road, Jangpura, **New Delhi**-110014. India

E-mail: *helpline@vikaspublishing.com* • Website: *www.vikaspublishing.com*

- **Ahmedabad** : 305, Grand Monarch, 100 ft Shyamal Road, Near Seema Hall, Ahmedabad-380051 • Ph. +91-79-65254204
- **Bengaluru** : First Floor, N S Bhawan, 4th Cross, 4th Main, Gandhi Nagar, Bengaluru-560009 • Ph. +91-80-22281254, 22204639
- **Chennai** : E-12, Nelson Chambers, 115, Nelson Manickam Road, Aminjikarai, Chennai-600029 • Ph. +91-44-23744547, 23746090
- **Hyderabad** : Aashray Mansion, Flat-G (G.F.), 3-6-361/8, Street No. 20, Himayath Nagar, Hyderabad-500029 • Ph.□+91-40-23269992 • Fax. +91-40-23269993
- **Kolkata** : 82, Park Street, Kolkata-700017 • Ph. +91-33-22837880
- **Mumbai** : 67/68, 3rd Floor, Aditya Industrial Estate, Chincholi Bunder, Behind Balaji International School & Evershine Mall, Malad (West), Mumbai-400064 • Ph. +91-22-28772545, 28768301
- **Patna** : Flat No. 101, Sri Ram Tower, Beside Chiraiyatand Over Bridge, Kankarbagh Main Rd., Kankarbagh, Patna-800020 • Ph. +91-612-2351147

How to Unblock Everything on the Internet
ISBN: 978-93259-6357-3

First Published 2012
Second Edition 2013
Reprinted in 2013
First Reprint 2014

Vikas® is the registered trademark of Vikas Publishing House Pvt Ltd
Copyright © Ankit Fadia, 2012, 2013

Information contained in this book has been published by VIKAS® Publishing House Pvt Ltd and has been obtained by its Authors from sources believed to be reliable and are correct to the best of their knowledge. However, the Publisher and its Authors shall in no event be liable for any errors, omissions or damages arising out of use of this information and specifically disclaim any implied warranties or merchantability or fitness for any particular use. Disputes if any are subject to Delhi Jurisdiction only.

Printed in India.

From the Press ...

'It's a little difficult to understand technology; however it's more difficult making others understand it. Ankit knows technology and he also knows how to explain it right ...'

Gaurav Upreti, Producer, Tech And You, NewsX

'A punch in the face of Internet Police ...'

HT City, Hindustan Times

'The Digital Hacktivist'

Mint

'Web of Knowledge'

The Tribune

'Fadia decodes secrets of social network'

The Asian Age

'Ankit Fadia roots for Freedom of Expression'

The Hindu

'Ethical Hacker tells how to beat censorship'

The Hindu Business Line

'Ethical Hacker Ankit Fadia steals the show'

The Bengal Post

'Hacks Off!'

The Economic Times, Madras Plus

'Top Ethical Hacker against Censor'

DNA

'Dousing the Firewalls'

The Deccan Chronicle

'Smooth Way to Surf'

Pune Mirror

'Call of the Hacker'

Sakaal Times

'What the hack!'

The New Indian Express

'Unblocking Freedom of Speech'

HT City, Chandigarh

'Key to Unlock Virtual World Is Out'

Hans India

'Govt. move on social networks' malicious content slammed'

Khaleej Times

'Shining White Hat to the Rescue'

Post Noon

This book is dedicated to a free and unblocked Internet

Contents

1 〉 Introduction

free·dom

- exemption from external control, interference, regulation, etc.

cen·sor

- an official who examines books, plays, news reports, motion pictures, radio and television programmes, letters, cablegrams, etc., for the purpose of suppressing parts deemed objectionable on moral, political, military, or other grounds.

- any person who supervises the manners or morality of others.

Internet censorship is defined as the control, filtration and restriction on access to information on the Internet. All of us have experienced censorship on the Internet in varied formats at different points in our lives. The earliest form of Internet censorship that many of us faced – maybe even without realizing it – was censorship of certain inappropriate websites on the Internet by our parents when we were kids. But doesn't matter, ignorance is bliss and it was probably the best thing for us as kids to be sheltered from the dark dangers of the Internet. Then as school students, we had restrictions put on the amount of time we were allowed access on the school computers and could only access a handful of websites that our teachers thought were appropriate.

With time, we grew older, left home for college, started living on our own away from our parents and started thinking of ourselves as adults who are capable of taking mature, independent decisions. Only to realize a few days into college that our college had blocked almost all the interesting websites on the Internet. Comparable to an orange with all its juice squeezed out, with only dry layered skin left behind for us to chew on. Doesn't matter, we are Indians. All throughout college we did some *jugaad* and anyhow managed to keep ourselves sane by trying to find some solace in the select few things that we were actually allowed to do on the Internet. Then, we slogged and slogged for several years, prepared for campus recruitments, fought our way through the mad race and finally landed ourselves nice jobs. Financial freedom, a visiting card with our name on it, not having to share a dirty bathroom with eight other guys and being able to splurge on some of life's luxuries was all so exciting. However, in office we suddenly realized that the restrictions that they were putting on our Internet activity were far bigger, stronger and superior than anything we had encountered before. The grass suddenly seemed much greener back in college. The restricted slow Internet access of our college days, which had earlier seemed like a prison sentence, now felt like a luxurious beach holiday.

But who were we to complain? After all, we live in ironical and funny times. We live in a country where in our early twenties we are allowed to drive, elect our government, marry and even drink alcohol, but all hell breaks loose if we want to check the latest cricket scores in the office or watch a video on YouTube! Doesn't matter, we adjusted like always. We restricted our time spent in the office to purely mindless robotic implementation of instructions given to us by our creator. I mean, our boss. We spent a major part of our twenties working hard, maybe got married, and bought a house on an EMI we knew we couldn't really afford, saved some money and then finally took the wife on a holiday to Dubai. We checked into an ostentatiously decorated five star hotel in Dubai with fantastic views from the floor to ceiling glass windows of our 82nd floor hotel room. This had to be heaven on earth. Wanting to show off this momentous occasion of joy to our friends and relatives we try to connect to Facebook on our laptop to upload pictures of the view of our room only to find that the Emirates government has blocked access to Facebook! Such is the restricted life on the Internet as we know it.

All traditional media (like television, newspapers, magazines, radio and others) in most countries have been regulated by the government for many years now. What makes regulation and censorship on the Internet a little more complicated is the fact that the Internet seamlessly crosses geographical boundaries. It is common for a user to be sitting in one country and accessing content hosted on a website located in another country. The content that is being accessed may be illegal and blocked in the country where the user is located, but may be completely legal, unblocked or unregulated in the country where the website is hosted. The extent of censorship of the Internet varies from country to country and within each country from organization to organization. For example, most western governments by and large provide their citizens with unblocked Internet access. On the other hand, many East Asian countries (like China, Myanmar, South Korea, Vietnam and others) and Middle Eastern countries (like UAE, Iran, Saudi Arabia and others) are actively blocking varying portions of the Internet. The reasons for blocking stuff on the Internet also vary quite widely ranging between some or all of these below reasons:

- **Security reasons:** Any content on the Internet that could pose a risk to the security of a country is normally blocked, censored or taken down by the government.

- **Legal reasons:** Illegal material like child pornography, piracy, copyright, gambling, violence, intellectual property theft and hate speech is usually blocked by governments, organizations and colleges as well. In the corporate world, in certain industries that may be working on sensitive data even websites which may be widely considered normal may be blocked due to legal and compliance reasons.

- **Economic interests:** Various governments, companies and hotels block access to websites that may hurt their selfish economic interests at the expense of the users. For example,

Skype, one of the most popular VOIP tools in the world, is blocked in various countries in the Middle East since its use leads to a loss of revenue for the local government-owned telecom providers. Although Skype is a lot cheaper and could help users save a lot of money, it is blocked to safeguard the economic interests of specific governments and companies.

- **Moral grounds:** Many governments and organizations like to take a high moral stance on perfectly legal websites which may have some controversial content and block them out.

- **Bandwidth purposes:** Many companies, organizations, colleges and even ISPs like to block certain websites that use more bandwidth than usual like video streaming websites, online music, gaming websites and many others.

- **Time & resources:** Many companies, organizations and colleges like to believe that if perfectly normal websites like Facebook, YouTube, Sports, News, Stocks and others are allowed to be accessed then everybody in the organization will end up wasting a lot of company time and resources.

- **Unusual events:** During the Arab Spring movements that took place across the MENA (Middle East and North Africa) region, various governments ended up blocking access to social networking sites like Facebook, Twitter and others. In some extreme cases, complete access to the Internet was taken away by governments.

When you try to access a blocked website, you will usually be shown an ACCESS DENIED error message, telling you that the website has been blocked by the respective government, company or college. Some governments and companies are very open and forthcoming about the websites and applications they are blocking. For example, many governments in the Middle East and various organizations in different parts of the world will explicitly tell their users that the website they are trying to access is blocked and sometimes they will even share the reason why it has been blocked.

On the other hand, several governments (like the Chinese government) and some organizations do not like to be forthcoming about the blocks that are in place. Instead of showing an error message when somebody tries to access a blocked website, they will instead simply redirect the user and show a fake NOT FOUND error message. Or they might even redirect the user to some other website which the user did not request but the government feels is appropriate for the user to view.

The things that get blocked on the Internet are quite diverse. Some of the most commonly blocked stuff on the Internet is:

- Social networking websites
- Video & audio streaming websites
- Sports websites
- Job Search websites
- Blogs
- Torrents
- Online gaming websites
- Instant messengers
- Web-based applications on your computer
- USB ports
- News websites

My personal opinion about Internet censorship and blocking by governments, companies and colleges is quite liberal. First of all, there is no question that illegal websites and content that threatens the security, peace and well-being of a country should obviously be blocked, censored, regulated or removed from the Internet. Also, in the corporate world, especially in sensitive industries due to legal or compliance reasons, if certain websites on the Internet need to be blocked, then they should be blocked. It is also best for governments, organizations and colleges to be upfront and open about their blocking policies with their users instead of trying to be secretive and vague about it. However, I strongly oppose any government action towards blocking of legal but controversial content on the Internet like political satire, humour and criticism. Similarly, I strongly oppose the move by companies, organizations and colleges to block perfectly legal and harmless websites like YouTube, Facebook, Orkut, sports and news sites.

Unfortunately, almost all colleges, companies and organizations across India enforce very strong and restrictive blocking rules on their users. Your favourite websites are blocked. You can't chat with your friends. You are not allowed to take a short break and watch funny videos on Youtube! You can't even keep a track of the latest cricket scores. Forget that, you are not allowed to even search without filters on Google. At the same time, our counterparts in western countries (on more occasions than not) have full unrestricted access to the Internet and are considered mature enough to handle this freedom responsibly. Are we less mature and responsible than them? Moreover, there is no research that proves that blocking access on the Internet increases productivity and profits of an organization or ensures that we do better in our educational or professional careers. In fact, people who anyway don't want to be responsible about their work and deadlines will not magically start working harder if their Internet privileges are taken away.

Different network administrators cite different reasons for blocking content on the Internet. Some network administrators cite the threat of security issues infiltrating their network if users are given unrestricted access to the Internet. However, in reality there are already reliable countermeasures (which do not require blocking content on the Internet) that are available to dispel any such security issues. And how come organizations and colleges in the western world who don't block anything on the Internet don't face security issues on their network? Some organizations cite bandwidth issues as the primary reason for blocking content on the Internet. Agreed, bandwidth can be expensive, but seriously how much bandwidth do most blocked websites really consume? Does accessing Facebook or watching a few minutes long YouTube videos really eat up that many resources? In the rare case, that the costs are putting an economic burden on the organization, then why not adopt a *freemium model,* where basic blocked Internet is available free of cost to users, but for unrestricted access a small fee is charged. Moreover on most occasions, if you notice a user spending a lot of time and resources on Web content they are not supposed to accesss, then a simple warning or counselling session should successfully resolve the matter. There is no need to completely ban or block websites on the Internet.

Colleges love to block Web 2.0 websites like Facebook, Twitter, Orkut, YouTube and other social networking websites citing the reason that users tend to waste a lot of time and resources on them. Do they really think that by unblocking such stuff, students will stop attending lectures, stop studying, stop worrying about their careers and spend the rest of their lives poking their friends on Facebook? We are tired of being treated like teenagers. Start treating us like adults, if you expect us to behave like adults. How come colleges in western countries do not block anything on the Internet and still produce excellent academic research and work?

We live in a very fast-paced interconnected world, where social media and Web 2.0 are an indispensable part of our daily lives as individuals and organizations. By blocking stuff on the Internet, networks are almost putting their users at a disadvantage as compared to users who have unrestricted Internet access. A blocked Internet is almost like cutting users off from their window to the world. For example, news is nowadays breaking first on Twitter and then on traditional news websites. In case of a natural calamity, the early warning advantage that Twitter and social media provide can actually save a lot of lives.

We are tired of these restrictions. We are demanding back our freedom. No, we are taking our freedom back with our own hands. We are not interested in breaking laws and accessing illegal content, we are only interested in having unrestricted access to legal content on the Internet. Let us and our Internet remain free.

How to Block Content on the Internet[*]

There is a variety of techniques, methods and tools that organizations, companies and colleges use to block content on the Internet. In this book, we will discuss them in detail, as well as the various ways in which you can circumvent them. But before going any further, there are some basic technical Internet-related terms that we must discuss so that the rest of the book is easy and straightforward to understand.

- **IP address:** Every computer connected to the Internet has a unique IP address given to it. An IP address is basically a computer's identity on the Internet at which it can be contacted. Think of it as the mobile phone number of your computer on the Internet, that is, a number at which it can be contacted on the Internet. Without knowing somebody else's IP address you cannot communicate on the Internet with that computer or server. Your computer has an IP address. Your friend's computer has an IP address and even all your favourite websites on the Internet have their own IP addresses. A typical IP address looks like the following: 203.14.11.12. You can find out your own computer's current IP address by simply starting your browser and connecting to the website http://www.whatismyipaddress.com.

---

* Reference: Wikipedia

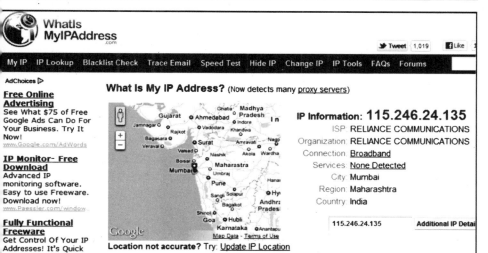

You can find out a website's IP address (let us assume google.com) by simply going to MSDOS or command line prompt (click on the Windows Start Orb button on the left bottom corner of the screen and type CMD in the quick search bar) and type the command *ping google.com*. Within a few seconds in the output, the IP address of google.com will be displayed. In this case, it happens to be 74.125.236.83.

```
C:\Users\ankitfadia>ping www.google.com

Pinging www.l.google.com [74.125.236.83] with 32 bytes of data:
Reply from 74.125.236.83: bytes=32 time=72ms TTL=57
Reply from 74.125.236.83: bytes=32 time=62ms TTL=57
Reply from 74.125.236.83: bytes=32 time=76ms TTL=57
Reply from 74.125.236.83: bytes=32 time=70ms TTL=57

Ping statistics for 74.125.236.83:
    Packets: Sent = 4, Received = 4, Lost = 0 (0% loss),
Approximate round trip times in milli-seconds:
    Minimum = 62ms, Maximum = 76ms, Average = 70ms

C:\Users\ankitfadia>
```

- **Domain name:** It is quite difficult to remember IP addresses since they are just a bunch of numbers. Imagine what a nightmare it would be if you had to remember and type an IP address in your browser each time you wanted to connect to any of your favourite websites. To make life simpler for users, every website not only has an IP address, but also has a corresponding domain name. A domain name is an easy-to-remember name for a website. For example, www.facebook.com is an example of a domain name. Unlike websites, usually home computers do not have a domain name.

- **Domain name system (DNS) lookups:** The process of converting a domain name into its respective IP address is known as a DNS lookup. Your browser performs a DNS lookup automatically in the background each time you type a website address (or domain) in your browser. Without a DNS lookup, a browser will not know the IP address of the website you wish to connect to and hence will not know how to connect to it.

- **Reverse DNS lookup:** It is the exact reverse process of converting an IP address into its respective domain name.

- **DNS server:** A DNS server is a server that handles DNS lookup queries from browsers/users and sends back replies to them. Typically, your college, company or organization will have its own DNS server that will manage the local user's DNS lookup requests.

- **HTTP** (stands for Hyper Text Transfer Protocol): It is the communication protocol that is normally used by your browser to communicate with websites. It contains all the rules that browsers follow to communicate with a remote website. The secure form of HTTP which allows users to have encrypted communicated with a websites is known as HTTPS.

- **Port:** A port is a door through which data enters or leaves your computer. Typically ports are used to exchange data between different devices. There are two types of ports:

- **Hardware ports**: All of us use hardware ports like USB ports, parallel ports, Ethernet port. These are normally used to exchange data between two devices.

- **Virtual ports:** All Web applications on your computer open something known as virtual ports on your computer to communicate with remote servers on the Internet. Without virtual ports there would be no way for applications on your computer to communicate with remote servers on the Internet. You can find a list of open virtual ports on your computer by simply going to the MSDOS prompt and typing the command *netstat –n.*

- **Proxy server:** A proxy server is a server or software that acts as an intermediary between a user and the Internet. Whenever a user sends a request for a webpage to a proxy server, the proxy server will forward that request to the relevant server on the Internet and then send back the response to the user. The working of a proxy server can be explained as given below:

  STEP 1: USER — sends request for a webpage — PROXY

  STEP 2: PROXY — sends same request to relevant website — WEBSITE

  STEP 3: WEBSITE — sends back requested page — PROXY

  STEP 4: PROXY — sends back request page — USER

Based on the above schematic, it is obvious that a proxy server can be used to protect one's identity on the Internet. Normally your computer will directly send a request to a website and the website will know your computer's identity or IP address. However, if you use a proxy server to send the request to a website, then the website will think that the proxy server is connecting to it, but in reality it is you who is using a proxy server to connect to a remote website anonymously.

Moreover, since a proxy server acts as an intermediary between a user and the Internet, it can be used to block access to some websites and prevent the user from connecting to them. A lot of governments, companies and colleges use a proxy server along with a list of banned websites to restrict access to some websites.

On the other hand, there are some proxy servers that do not restrict or block access to any website on the Internet. So many users instead of connecting to the proxy server of their office or college will simply connect to a proxy server that does not block anything to gain uncensored access to the entire Internet.

Although there are different types of proxy servers available on the Internet, the most popular types are the following:

- **Web proxy or HTTP proxy:** It is a type of a proxy server that primarily is used to connect users with websites on the Internet using the HTTP protocol. Usually, a web proxy server will accept the requested web address in an input box within the browser window.

- **DNS proxy:** It is a type of proxy server that takes the DNS queries from the browser on a local network and forwards them to the nearest DNS server.

- **SOCKS proxy:** It is a type of a proxy server that allows users to connect to a remote server using all different protocols like TCP, UDP, FTP, etc. Its use is not just restricted to giving users access to websites.

There are different techniques that are used by governments, companies and colleges to censor the Internet and block access to websites and content on the Internet:

- **Domain name filtering**: Whenever you type a domain name in your browser, a DNS lookup query is sent to the local DNS server. It may be possible for a college or company to block DNS lookups for some domain names. If a browser cannot perform a DNS lookup for a particular domain, then it cannot access it. For example, if a network blocks DNS lookups for the Gmail server and the Google Talk server, then you will not be able to use your browser to connect to Gmail, nor will you be able to use your Google Talk Instant Messenger application since it will not be able to connect to the Google Talk server.

- **IP address filtering:** In such a filtering technique, instead of blocking domain names at the DNS server level, access to certain IP addresses are blocked by the network administrator.

- **Proxy filtering:** A lot of organizations will make all users connect to the Internet via a proxy server. The proxy server will monitor all the websites that users are trying to access and can be configured to block or redirect a user in case they try to access a website that the organization chooses to block.

- **URL filtering:** In such a filtering technique, the entire URL address is scanned for certain blocked domains or keywords. In case any blocked domain or keyword is found, then the user is blocked and denied access to the respective website.

- **Port blocking:** In order to function properly, some web applications open certain predefined local ports on your machine or establish outgoing connections to certain predefined ports on the remote machine. Without this, the applications cannot function and communicate on the Internet. To block the use of some applications, many network administrators will simply block the respective ports it uses to function. Such a technique effectively blocks the use of those respective applications. For example, to block the use of applications like Torrents and Skype, port blocking is commonly used.

- **Advance packet filtering:** In such a filtering technique, the transmission between a user and a remote website is monitored for certain keywords and as soon as any blocked keywords are detected, then the connection is reset or disconnected.

- **Limits:** Some organizations like to limit the amount of data a particular user can download in a predefined time period. As soon as that limit is reached, then the user's access to the Internet is taken away. Instead of a data limit, some organizations also put a time limit on the Internet access of a user.

- **Complete disconnection:** This is normally seen only in case of emergency or unusual situations when a government disconnects users from the Internet completely by removing the link between the users and the Internet.

- **Filtered access:** Many governments and organizations will allow users to search for only certain keywords on Google or access only specificvideos on YouTube. This filtered access is also a commonly used blocking mechanism.

Now that we know how organizations block content on the Internet, let us see some of the most commonly used techniques to unblock everything on the Internet.

3 Cached Pages

All popular search engines like Google, Bing, Yahoo and others spider the entire Internet, recording all metadata details and keywords that appear on all the pages. This recorded metadata and keywords of all the web pages are then used to determine a page's quality and rank in the search results (along with multiple other criteria). Along with recording metadata and keywords, most search engines also take a snapshot of all webpages on the Internet and store a cache copy of them. This can be extremely useful for users who are stuck behind company, college or government firewalls and are not allowed to access certain websites.

Imagine that there is a particular website that you really want to access but unfortunately the website has gone down. Or imagine some content that was published on a website, which was then taken down a few days later for some reason. If you still wish to see that content, you can try viewing a cached copy of the webpage on a search engine. Not only that, sometimes your company, college or government firewall may have blocked access to a particular webpage, but you may still be able to access it by viewing a cached copy of it on a search engine!

Typically, whenever you search for some keywords on popular search engines like Google, Bing or Yahoo, then below or next to each search result you will see a *Cached* link that will allow you to view the most recent cached copy of that particular webpage. This option is very useful for viewing webpages that have been taken down for some reason or are blocked by your college or company. For example, let us assume that your college or company has blocked access to the Kolaveri Di Wikipedia page, but you really want to access it. All you have to do is:

STEP 1: Start your browser and connect to any popular search engine of your choice. I am going to use Google for this example.

STEP 2: Search for the blocked webpage that you wish to access. (In this case I am going to search for the keywords 'why this kolaveri di wikipedia'.

Within the search results that get displayed, look for the relevant blocked webpage that you wish to access and click on the CACHED link below it or next to it to access its cached copy. On Google, in case you do not see the CACHED link below the search results, then you need to move your mouse over the instant preview button next to the search result and then on the right hand side preview space, the CACHED link will appear. The best part about this technique is that your network will think that you are simply accessing Google (which may not be blocked), but in reality you are using the search engine to access blocked content. As simple as that!

When you click on the cached link of a search result, then within a few seconds, Google will open the most recent cached copy of that page and display it for you. Irrespective of whether that page may be currently down or may have been blocked by your network, you are still able to see it.

It is also possible to directly view a cached copy of a particular webpage or URL by using simple search operators on Google. For example, on Google if you were to search for *cache: www.timesofindia.com*, it will automatically display the most recent cached copy of the Times Of India home page.

When you are viewing a cached page, typically Google will mention at the top the date and time from which the cached copy is being displayed. This may vary from webpage to webpage, depending upon how often Google spiders that respective webpage. It is also possible for a web developer to specify that Google should not cache its webpage and in such a case the CACHE link or the cache operator may not work or may just display the most current version of the webpage.

Accessing a cached page instead of the actual page is a simple but clever trick of fooling the local firewall, bypassing any basic filters that may be in place and accessing content that may have been blocked! Unfortunately, such an unblocking technique remains quite basic and easily detected and blocked. The problem is that when you access the cached page of a blocked website, then the URL that gets displayed in your browser still contains the blocked domain name. Hence, such a technique can easily be blocked by a smart network administrator.

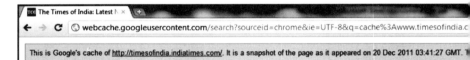

4 > Archived Pages

The cache pages and links on search engines give the most recent cached version of a webpage. However, sometimes you may want to access an even older version of the same webpage for research purposes or just out of curiosity. If you want to see what a webpage looked like several years ago, then there is a very cool tool called the WAYBACKMACHINE that is available for free at www.archive.org. Since the year 1996, archive.org has been spidering the Internet with the intention of creating a permanent digital library of the Internet for researchers, historians and the general public. This is a fantastic tool that allows you to search for and view an old archived version of popular webpages on the Internet from several months or even years back!

If you are thinking what I am thinking, then you probably realize that not only can this be very useful for research purposes, it can also be used to unblock webpages that may have been blocked by your local network. Most companies and colleges will not have blocked access to the WAYBACKMACHINE tool and once you connect to it, you can easily use it to access some other blocked website. Your local firewall thinks that you are accessing an unblocked website (WayBackMachine), but in reality you are using it to connect to a blocked website. As simple as that! In the screenshots below, we are going to see how easy it is for you to use the WAYBACKMACHINE tool to view a cached copy of the www.timesofindia.com website from the year 2001.

STEP 1: Start your browser and connect to www.archive.org, type the website URL whose cached or archived copy you wish to view in the space provided and click on the TAKE ME BACK button. For example, www.timesofindia.com

STEP 2: Select the year, month and date from which you wish to view the archived copy. In this example, we are going to pretend that we want to see the March 5, 2001 copy of the www.timesofindia.com website.

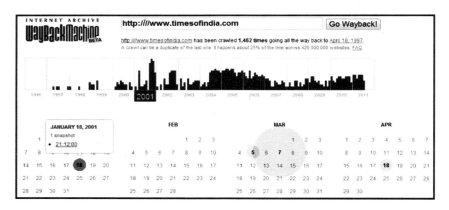

STEP 3: Within a few seconds, the WAYBACKMACHINE tool will display the archived copy of the www.timesofindia.com website from the date that you selected in the previous step.

The WAYBACKMACHINE software is very useful to access popular websites that may have been blocked. However, it cannot be used to access blocked websites that may not be that popular or websites that have dynamic content (like YouTube, Facebook, etc). Moreover, whenever you are on the WAYBACKMACHINE website to access an archive copy of a blocked webpage, the blocked domain still appears in the browser URL bar. Most importantly, this is just one website and can easily be blocked by your network administrator.

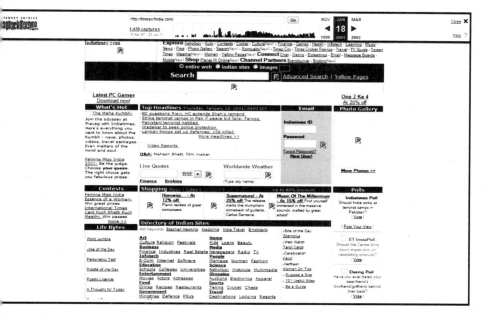

Translation Tools

There are various free translation websites available that allow users to translate text and webpages from one language to another on the Internet. For example, if you wish to read a webpage or document that has been written in Japanese and the only language that you can read is Hindi, then you can use a translation website to translate the text from Japanese to Hindi on the fly. All for free! The two most popular translations tools on the Internet are:

- **Google Translate** (http://translate.google.com): provides instant translation between 58 different languages.
- **Yahoo Babelfish** (http://babelfish.yahoo.com): supports fewer languages but still does a decent job.

The technology behind the instant translation of webpages is obviously quite cool. But what is even cooler is the fact that it is possible to use these translation websites to unblock websites and access censored content!

Let us assume that your college or company has blocked access to the YouTube website and you are shown the blocked error message each time you try to access it. However, if you experiment a little bit, you may realize that your network may not have actually blocked access to the websites of Google Translate or Yahoo BabelFish. This means that it may be possible for you to connect to either of these translation websites and use them to access YouTube by translating it from English to any other language of your choice, including Hindi, Tamil, Bengali and various other regional Indian languages (Indian regional languages are supported only by Google Translate). Your college or company thinks that you are accessing a safe unblocked website (the translation website), but in reality you are using the translation website to access a blocked website! Below we will see how easy it is for you to use Google Translate to access a blocked YouTube video:

STEP 1: Start your browser and connect to http://translate.google.com so that your local firewall thinks that you are connecting to a safe normal, unblocked website. In the space provided, type the web address of the blocked website that you wish to access. In this case, we are going to type www.youtube.com. Then select the original language of the webpage (in this case English) and the language into which you wish to translate the web page (in this case, Hindi). Finally, click on the Translate button.

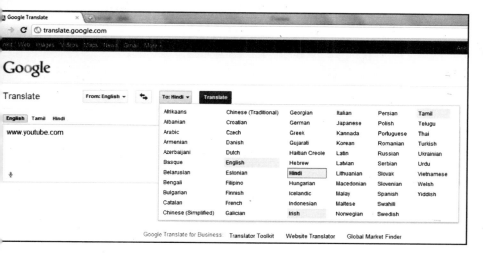

STEP 2: Within a few seconds, the Hindi translated version of the YouTube website will get displayed on the screen. The fact of the matter is that even though the website has been translated into Hindi, the interface is still the same and the actual language of the videos that you are going to watch will remain the same. In other words, an English video will always remain an English video even if the YouTube interface is displayed in Hindi or some other language. The best part is your college or company thinks you are accessing a Google Translation website, which is far from reality. Go ahead and try it out. It is important to note that when you use

the Google Translate service, some of the links or search features on the translated page may not work.

STEP 3: You can navigate to the page of the video that you wish to watch by clicking on the links on the YouTube home page or if you know the direct URL of the video you wish to watch, then you can directly type it into the translate input box at the top of your browser and you will be directly taken to the video. The video will play normally as it is supposed to play and will be in its original language; only the interface language will change.

The problem with such translation websites is that the requested domain of the blocked website appears in plaintext in the browser URL address bar and that makes it easy for system administrators to block it. Moreover, there are only two popular and effective translation websites on the Internet, which means that they can both be blocked.

Google translate http://www.youtube.com/watch?v=YR12Z8f1Dh8

From: English ▼ To: Hindi ▼ Translate

क्यों इस Kolaveri डि पूर्ण HD में गाने के प्रोमो वीडियो

sonymusicindiaSME ⊕ सदस्यता 464 वीडियो ▼

To set the songs of *Three* as your Caller Ring Back Tone Dial 04466886600

Flop song . .

0:14 / 4:09 360p + YouTube

👍 जैसा 👎 + जोड़ें ▼ शेयर ⚑ 20,341,650 ▥

दवारा अपलोड की sonymusicindiaSME 16 नवम्बर, 2011 को 169,257 पसंद है, 8526 नापसंद

चिन्ना आश्चर्य 👁 के रूप में:

इस अनन्य संगीतकार अनिरुद्ध, धनुष, श्रुति हसन, ऐश्वर्या और साउंड इंजीनियर शिवकुमार भारत रीमल टाइम

के साथ गीत की रिकॉर्डिंग के दौरान शॉट वीडियो बाहर की जाँच करें पर देखा

Format Conversion Websites

6

There are numerous conversion websites available on the Internet that can convert a website into different formats. It is possible to use these websites to access blocked websites on the Internet. For example, there is a website called http://pdfmyurl.com, which converts any URL into a PDF document and allows users to download it. For example, let us assume that the BBC website (http://www.bbc.co.uk/) is blocked in your company or college, but you want to read a news story on this website. In such a scenario, all you have to do is use the website PDF MY URL to convert the blocked webpage on the Internet into its respective PDF version.

STEP 1: Open your browser and connect to http://pdfmyurl.com/ and type the URL that you want to convert into a PDF document in the space provided. In this case I have typed the website address www.bbc.co.uk.

STEP 2: Within a few seconds, the website PDF MY URL will allow you to download a PDF version of the requested webpage, which you can download and read even though the requested URL may be blocked by your local firewall.

Similarly, there is another website http://www.url2png.com/ which allows users to convert a webpage into a PNG format image. This website can also be used to access blocked websites on the Internet by fooling the local firewall. Another cool website that allows you take snapshots of various websites on the Internet is http://browsershots.org.

Unfortunately, like the translation or archiving websites, these format conversion websites can easily be blocked as well.

Webpages through Email

Imagine that there is a website on which there is some text or content that you want to access. Unfortunately, your college or company or government has set up a firewall or filtering device that has blocked access to it. But you still really want to access the data or content on that website. What do you do? This is where a fantastic service of accessing webpages via email comes into the picture. All you have to do is simply send the web address that you want to access via email to a predefined email address and a few minutes later the requested web page will be emailed back to you. The most popular websites that allow you to request blocked web pages via email are the following:

- **www4mail (http://www.www4mail.org):** To request a web page via email through this website you need to send an email to www4mail@wm.ictp.trieste.it and the subject can be blank and in the body of the email you need to write the requested web page address.

- **Web2Mail (http://www.web2mail.com/):** To request a web page via email through this website you need to first register for free on their website and then send an email from the registered email account to www@web2mail.com and in the subject of the email write the URL of the web page that you wish to request.

NOTE: You can expect unreliable results with both these websites, since they are no longer fully supported. I tested both these websites several times while doing research for this book.

While they were working fine sometimes, on some occasions they simply did not work.

For example, to request the webpage http://www.samair.ru/proxy/type-01.htm via email using the www4mail website, the following steps need to be followed:

(This requested web page contains a list of proxy servers that can be used to bypass the firewall in your college or company. We will be discussing proxy servers later on in this book. This webpage is normally blocked by your college or company firewall.)

STEP 1: Log into your email account and send an email to www4mail@wm. ictp.trieste.it where the subject is left blank and in the body of the email, the requested web page address is written: http://www.samair.ru/proxy/type-01.htm

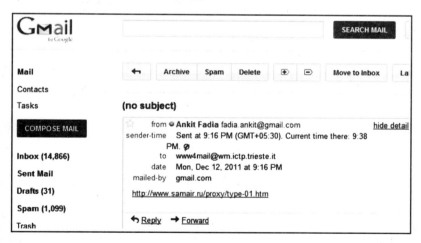

STEP 2: Wait for a few minutes after which you will receive an email from www4mail with the requested webpage included as an attachment.

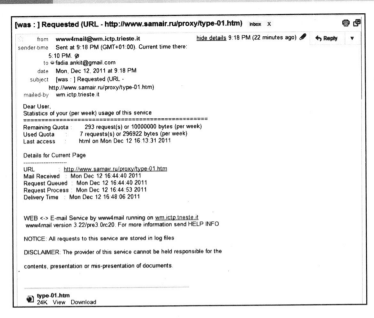

STEP 3: You can open the attachment to view the contents of the requested web page. As simple as that! In this case when I open the attachment, the contents of the requested page show up on the screen, which in this case happens to be a list of proxy servers which can be used to bypass censorship and filtering. We will discuss proxy servers in detail later in this book.

IP address	Anonymity level	Checked time	Country
$6.50/month	£5.00/month	€5.00/month	€5.0/month
117.55.195.102:8080	transparent proxy	169 minutes ago	Afghanistan
117.55.195.42:8080	transparent	81 minutes ago	Afghanistan
196.20.65.211:8080	anonymous	54 minutes ago	Algeria
190.105.88.92:8080	transparent	19 minutes ago	Argentina
201.216.236.117:80	high-anonymous	95 minutes ago	Argentina
200.58.99.97:80	anonymous proxy	118 minutes ago	Argentina
201.216.234.9:8080	anonymous proxy	146 minutes ago	Argentina
200.58.99.94:80	anonymous	175 minutes ago	Argentina
	Reliable Anonymous Proxy!		
200.51.203.200:80	anonymous proxy	146 minutes ago	Argentina
113.192.1.99:80	transparent proxy server	86 minutes ago	Australia
115.124.0.4:8080	transparent proxy	117 minutes ago	Australia
113.192.1.99:3128	transparent proxy	117 minutes ago	Australia
85.126.224.146:8080	transparent proxy	80 minutes ago	Austria
81.223.73.243:80	anonymous server	146 minutes ago	Austria

USA Proxy Server - UK Proxy Server - Proxy Server France - German Proxy Server

1 2 3 4 5 6 7 8 9 10 11 12 13 14 15 16 17 18 19 20 21 next

8 > URL Shortening Websites

In the world of Twitter and Instant messaging, where length of characters is a major restriction, shortening of web address URLs has become very popular. URL shortening is the technique that allows users to access a particular webpage using its equivalent shortened address instead of the actual web address. Not only does URL shortening make a URL much shorter, it also makes it easier to remember. Popular URL shortening websites include www.bit.ly, www.tiny.cc, www.goo.gl and www.tinyurl.com.

URL shortening means that instead of typing the original long URL in the browser address bar, users now have to only type its shortened version. The browser will send an HTTP request to the shortened URL server, which will then send back an HTTP redirect message to the user, redirecting the user to the actual website. Since the initial outgoing HTTP request from the user is going to the URL shortening website and not the actual website that the user is trying to access, it means that such a technique can also be used to bypass the local firewall.

Let us assume that www.facebook.com is blocked by your network, then it is possible for the user to continue to access it by shortening the URL with the help of any of the numerous URL shortening websites. Once the shortened URL is created, then instead of typing www.facebook.com in the browser, if the user simply types the shortened URL, then he should technically be able to access the Facebook website. The local firewall thinks that the user is trying to access the URL shortening website, but in reality, the user is using this technique to connect to a blocked website.

STEP 1: To create a shortened URL, simply start your browser and connect to any URL shortening website. My favourite URL shortening website is goo.gl. Once you are connected to it, simply type the URL you wish to shorten in the space provided and click on the Shorten button. Within a few seconds, the website will display the shortened URL, which can easily be copied to your clipboard.

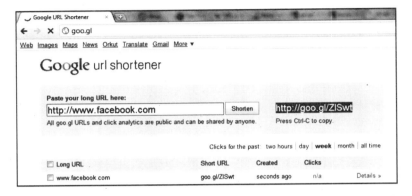

STEP 2: Copy and paste the shortened URL into any browser window and you will be taken to Facebook.com.

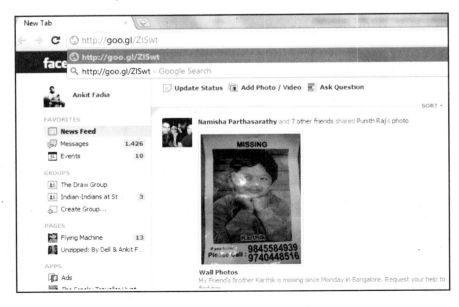

However, it is important to note that such shortened URLs can easily be misused by a criminal to redirect the victim to malicious websites for phishing, stealing and other purposes, since by simply reading the URL or even hovering the mouse over the shortened URL, it is not possible for a user to find out the real destination of the link. From a security perspective, it is always a good idea for users to preview a link before opening or viewing it in the browser. Different URL shortening websites have different ways to preview its URL as described in the below table:

URL Shortening Website	How to Preview a URL
http://Bit.ly	Add a + after the URL
http://goo.gl	Visit www.longurl.org
http://tiny.cc/	Add a = sign after the URL
http://www.tinyurl.com	Add a preview. after http://

9 Website Aliases

Normally you have to type the domain name of a website in your browser to be able to access it. Domain names are usually easy to remember and can be easily read by human beings. The browser then sends the domain name you type to the local Domain Name Server (DNS) Server to convert it into its respective IP address. This process of converting a domain name into its respective IP address is known as a DNS lookup query. Once the browser knows the IP address of the domain name you typed, it then sends an HTTP request to that IP address asking for the webpage that you wish to view. That is how a website is typically displayed on your computer.

The DNS server to which your browser sends the DNS lookup query is normally controlled by your company, college, ISP or government. This means that it is possible for them to monitor all the DNS lookup requests that they receive and block DNS lookup requests for certain websites. For example, they could have a filtering mechanism in place which looks for any DNS lookups for the domain www.facebook.com and as soon as they receive it, they will block the user and send back an ACCESS DENIED error message. Such a practice will prevent the user from being able to access the Facebook website.

If you land up in a situation where your college or company is blocking websites by monitoring and blocking DNS lookup queries, then worry not; it is actually quite easy for you to continue to access your favourite blocked websites on the Internet. Instead of typing the domain name of the blocked website that you want to access, all you have to do is to simply type its respective IP address. If you do not type a domain name in your browser, then no DNS lookup query is sent to the DNS server of your company, college, ISP or government. Instead your browser directly sends the HTTP request to the website that you wish to access. Since the DNS lookup step gets skipped, any filtering or blocking that might have been implemented at the DNS lookup level by your network will no longer work and you will be able to access all your favourite websites.

STEP 1: Let us assume that you wish to access www.google.com, but when you directly type its domain in your browser, you are shown the ACCESS DENIED error message. In such a scenario, it is recommended that instead you should try typing the respective IP address of google.com.

STEP 2: Start MSDOS or the command line prompt (Click on the Windows ORB logo on the left bottom corner of your screen and type *cmd* in the search field) and type the following ping command to convert the domain www.google.com to its respective IP address (in this case, we clearly know that the IP address that google.com resolves to is 74.125.246.80):

C:\Users\ankitfadia>ping www.google.com

Pinging www.l.google.com [74.125.236.80] with 32 bytes of data:

Reply from 74.125.236.80: bytes=32 time=64ms TTL=57

Reply from 74.125.236.80: bytes=32 time=62ms TTL=57

Reply from 74.125.236.80: bytes=32 time=61ms TTL=57

Reply from 74.125.236.80: bytes=32 time=60ms TTL=57

Ping statistics for 74.125.236.80:

Packets: Sent = 4, Received = 4, Lost = 0 (0% loss),

Approximate round trip times in milli-seconds:

Minimum = 60ms, Maximum = 64ms, Average = 61ms

STEP 3: Open your browser and instead of typing www.google.com, simply type its respective IP address and if everything goes well you will be able to bypass the filtering mechanism of your network and access the Google website! I tested this technique on three of the most popular browsers on the Internet (Mozilla Firefox, Google Chrome and Internet Explorer) and all of them supported it.

On many occasions your local network administrator may have blocked the PING command and you may not be able to use it convert a domain to its respective IP address. In such a case, you can use any of the numerous online ping tool interfaces that are available. For example, there is a very cool website called www.ping.eu, which allows you to perform PING straight from your browser even if it is blocked by your local network.

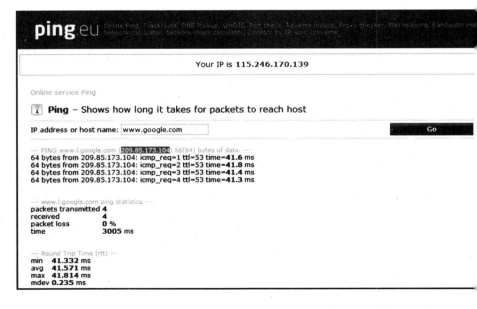

If you notice the above screenshot carefully, you will notice that the IP address that www.google.com resolves to using the website www.ping.eu is different from the IP address that it resolves to when you use ping on your computer. In case of ping.eu, Google resolves to the IP address 209.85.173.104 and in case of the ping tool on my machine, it resolved to 74.125.246.80. This difference in IP address is because Google has servers in different parts of the world and depending upon your location you are taken to different servers. Since the Ping.eu server is located somewhere in Europe, when you ping Google the IP address that is returned is different from what it resolves to when you ping Google from your own computer. But the best part is, typing either of the IP addresses will work! This means that if your local administrator has become a little smart and is not only blocking www.google.com, but is also blocking 74.125.246.80, then you can still access Google by typing its European Server IP address 209.85.173.104!

Hence, if typing a domain name does not give you access to it, then simply try typing its respective IP address and you may actually be allowed to access the blocked website! A domain name and its respective IP address both take a user to the same website.

Every system that is connected to the Internet has a unique IP address associated with it, which becomes its identity at which it can be contacted. Typically an IP address is a 32-bit number that is written in the dotted-decimal notation. For example, the dotted-decimal IP address of google.co.in is:

74.125.236.80

A smart system administrator will not only block the domain google.com but will also block its respective IP address at the firewall level, hence, making it a lot tougher for a user to unblock access.

It is important to note that it is possible to write a dotted-decimal IP address in various different formats. If your local network has blocked the decimal dotted IP address of a particular website, then you maybe try typing the IP address in decimal (no dots) format. There is a very cool website called http://www.allredroster.com/iptodec.htm that allows you to convert a dotted decimal IP address into a no dots decimal IP address.

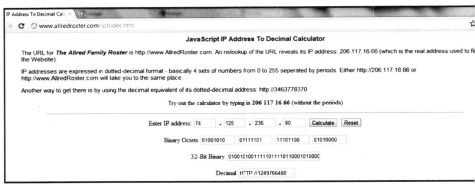

This means that if your system administrator has blocked www.google.com, then you can try typing its respective decimal dotted IP address http://74.125.236.80 and if that is blocked too, then you even try typing the decimal no dots version of the address HTTP://1249766480. All three are merely different ways of writing the same address and all three technically point you to the same website and may be used to bypasses local firewall filters and blocking mechanisms.

It is also possible to convert a decimal dotted IP address into its respective Octal format to bypass local firewalls and blocks. This conversion is possible using the Windows Calculator or using any of the various online conversion tools (use google to find them). A quick search and conversion reveals that the IP address 74.125.236.80 converts to 0112.0175.0354.0120 in its octal format (please note that in the octal format you have to precede each octal number with a 0 to tell the browser that the address is in octal format):

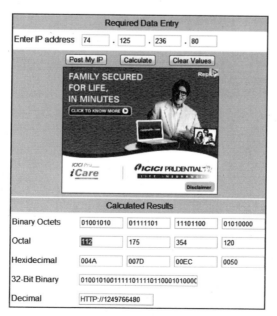

Most browsers accept IP addresses written in the octal format as well and your local firewall blocking is also circumvented. In other words, www.google.com, http://74.125.236.80, HTTP://1249766480 and http://0112.0175.0354.0120 all point to the same website.

It doesn't end here. It is also possible to convert a decimal format IP address into is respective hexadecimal format to bypass the filtering mechanism of your local network. The easiest way to convert a decimal IP address into its respective hexadecimal format is to use the Windows calculator. Let us assume that you want to convert the IP address 74.125.236.80 (Google) into its respective hexadecimal format then simply follow the below steps:

STEP 1: Start the Windows Calculator and click on VIEW > PROGRAMMER. Make sure decimal option is selected in the left column. Type the first decimal number into the calculator. In this case, I type 74.

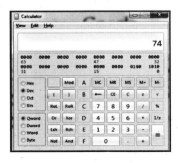

STEP 2: Now click on the HEX option in the left column. This will automatically convert the number you entered in decimal format, that is, 74, into the hexadecimal format, that is, 4A:

STEP 3: Repeat this exercise for all the decimals in the IP address and you will get the respective hexadecimal address, which in this case will be: 4A.7D.EC.50. Whenever you write an IP address in the hexadecimal format, then you have to precede each number with 0x to denote that it is in hex format. Hence, the hexadecimal address becomes: 0x4A.0x7D.0xEC. 0x50.

STEP 4: Start your browser and type the hexadecimal address (http://0x4A.0x7D.0xEC.0x50) of the Google website to fool the local firewall and access it! In other words, www.google.com, http://74.125.236.80, HTTP://1249766480, http://0112.0175.0354.0120 and (http://0x4A.0x7D.0xEC.0x50 all point to the same website.

It is also possible to convert an IP address into its respective binary format, but unfortunately most browsers do not support binary format addresses.

Another cool thing that you can do with IP addresses is to write them in hybrid format by combining multiple formats into one. For example, the various address formats of Google.com are

Dotted Decimal Format: http://74.125.236.80

No dots Decimal Format: HTTP://1249766480

Octal Format: http://0112.0175.0354.0120

Hexadecimal Format: http://0x4A.0x7D.0xEC.0x50

It is possible to access google.com by typing a combination of the above mentioned various formats. For example, http://74.0175.0xEC.80 (which is a combination of decimal, octal and hex formats) points to the same Google website!

Sometimes it is also a good idea for you to try different versions of the domain name itself to try and fool the firewall into giving you access. For example, sometimes www.facebook.com may be blocked, but it may be worthwhile to try any of the below alternatives, which all point to the same website and may allow you to unblock blocked websites:

www.facebook.com/; facebook.com; facebook.com/

https://www.facebook.com/index.php

https://www.facebook.com/index.php/

10 Special URLs

Sometimes it is possible to thwart the filtering mechanism of your local firewall by using special URL or web addresses which are specifically designed with the intention of fooling the firewall into letting you access a blocked website. There is no guarantee that the techniques discussed in this section will work each and every time, but there is no harm trying.

A lot of times, when http://www.facebook.com is blocked by your network administrator, then it is possible to unblock it by typing www.www.www.www. www.www.facebook.com in your browser.

This will most likely show an SSL certificate error message, which you can ignore and continue to access your blocked website. By typing the additional www's it becomes possible to bypass a bunch of different firewalls and blocks.

Within a few seconds you will be able to access the actual Facebook website which will look the below:

Another technique of fooling some of the firewalls and filtering mechanisms is to type a URL web address like the following:

http://www.iitd.ac.in@www.facebook.com

In such a URL web address, everything before the '@' sign is ignored and what actually gets loaded on the screen is the Facebook website.

RSS Aggregators

Many blogs, news sites, sports and other websites whose content changes quite regularly will make something known as an RSS feed available to users. An RSS feed is a subscription to a website through which users can automatically access any updated or new content that may be available. RSS feeds can be read using RSS readers or aggregators like Google Reader (http://reader.google. com).

There have been many occasions in the past where a government or organization has blocked access to a blog or newspaper or media house that is deemed to be controversial. In such a case, if you try using your browser to connect to the controversial website, then you will be denied access. However, if you want to continue to access the content on the blocked website, then it may be possible for you to subscribe to the RSS feed of that website using any popular RSS aggregator (my favourite is the Google Reader RSS aggregator). Usually, a government, company, college or ISP would only block direct access to a website, but it may not be possible for them to block access to the RSS feed of a website without blocking the complete RSS aggregator. For example, let us assume that your government has blocked access to cnn.com because it published some controversial story and it is no longer possible to access www.cnn.com using your browser. But you really want to find a way to access the articles on the CNN websites which have been blocked. In such a scenario, you can do is the following:

STEP 1: Start your browser and connect to the Google Reader website (http://reader.google.com)

STEP 2: You can search for any RSS feeds that you want to subscribe to by typing in the relevant keywords. In this example, I want to access content from the blocked CNN website, so I search for the keyword CNN and subscribe to their official RSS feed:

STEP 3: Now the Google Reader allows me to read the latest news stories from the CNN website, even though officially, the CNN website has been blocked by the local government or company or ISP.

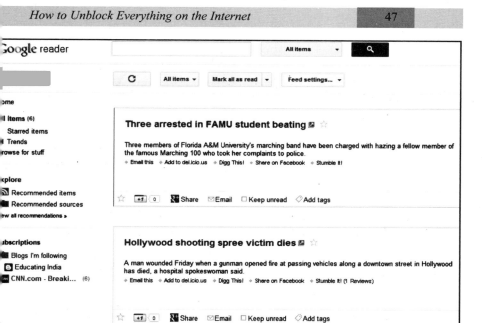

This technique will only work for those websites that have an RSS feed option available.

<table>
<tr><td>12</td><td># Mobile Websites</td></tr>
</table>

Most system administrators nowadays block popular websites like YouTube, Facebook, Google and so on. However, a very simple yet effective way of unblocking access to these websites is to simply start your browser and try to connect to the mobile versions of these popular websites. If your system administrator is blocking websites only based on specific addresses, then such an unblocking strategy will work quite effectively in giving you access. Most of the popular websites that are normally blocked by companies and colleges have a mobile version that you can try to use:

YouTube - http://m.youtube.com/

Facebook - http://m.facebook.com/

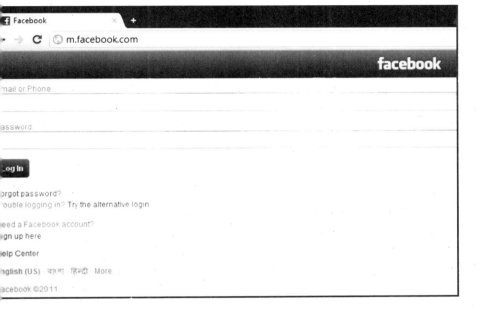

Google - http://www.google.com/mobile/

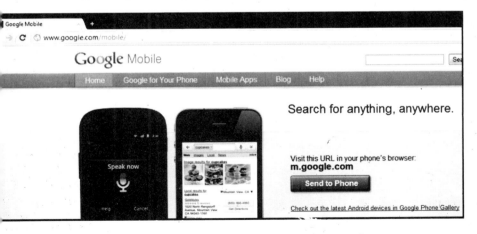

Twitter - http://m.twitter.com

CricInfo - http://m.espncricinfo.com/

The only problem with this technique is that not all websites have mobile versions available and even if they do, such a technique is relatively easy to block by a system administrator.

13   HTTP Secure

HTTP stands for Hypertext Transfer Protocol, and it is the protocol most commonly used by your browser to request web pages from servers on the Internet. It is the de facto protocol that is used by clients (users) to communicate with servers (websites). Whenever you type a web address in your browser, the HTTP protocol kicks in and does things in the background that eventually displays the requested page on your screen. The HTTP protocol normally requests the webpage you want to access by connecting to Port 80 of the remote server and the web address is preceded by http://.

It is quite easy for your college or company to block outgoing HTTP requests to Port 80 of any website of their choice. For example, it is quite easy for them to use a firewall or filtering device to monitor all outgoing HTTP requests sent to Port 80 of a remote server and then block any requests that are being sent to specific websites like http://www.facebook.com or http://www.orkut.com or http://www.youtube.com. If such a filtering is implemented, it would mean that you would not be allowed to access these websites! This is where a simple solution that makes use of the HTTP Secure protocol comes into the picture.

HTTP Secure, or HTTPS, is basically a combination of regular HTTP protocol and SSL encryption protocol. It allows a user to establish a secure encrypted connection with a website hosted on a remote server. Typically, HTTPS is a protocol that is commonly used by websites with sensitive transactions like online payments. Other than being secure, another difference between https and http is the fact that by default, https connects to Port 443 of the remote server and the web address is preceded by https://.

A number of careless or inexperienced system administrators will only block outgoing HTTP requests that are going to Port 80 of a website and will forget to block outgoing HTTPS requests that are going to Port 443 of the same website. This means that if http://www.google.com is blocked by your system administrator, you could try to unblock it by simply changing the protocol and remote port number being accessed by typing https://www.facebook.com. On many occasions this simple trick will do the job and will allow you to access blocked websites. As simple as that!

Normally, when you are connecting to websites using HTTP protocol, your computer will connect to Port 80 of the remote websites. There is a simple command line or MSDOS tool called *netstat* that displays all the current active connections on your computer, including the remote address and port numbers on which they are established. When you are connected to remote websites merely using HTTP and if you go to the MSDOS prompt and type the command *netstat –n* you will get the following reply (It is important to note that *netstat –n* tells you that most of the remote ports that you are connected to on remote machines are on Port 80, that is, HTTP port.)

C:\Users\ankitfadia>netstat -n

Active Connections

Proto	Local Address	Foreign Address	State
TCP	115.246.91.136:1073	174.132.196.42:80	ESTABLISHED
TCP	115.246.91.136:1231	124.124.252.51:80	CLOSE_WAIT
TCP	115.246.91.136:2514	85.24.189.121:18887	ESTABLISHED
TCP	115.246.91.136:2586	85.24.189.121:9222	ESTABLISHED
TCP	115.246.91.136:2600	124.124.252.11:80	ESTABLISHED

TCP	115.246.91.136:2602	124.124.252.17:80	ESTABLISHED
TCP	115.246.91.136:2604	46.28.109.169:8445	ESTABLISHED
TCP	115.246.91.136:2610	74.125.236.55:443	ESTABLISHED
TCP	127.0.0.1:31000	127.0.0.1:32000	ESTABLISHED
TCP	127.0.0.1:32000	127.0.0.1:31000	ESTABLISHED

Now if you were to close all browser windows and just connect to https://www.facebook.com and quickly open up MSDOS or the Command Line prompt and type the netstat –n command, you will notice that almost all outgoing connections are now connected to Port 443 (the HTTPS Port) on the remote servers. This is the main difference between HTTP and HTTPS.

C:\Users\ankitfadia>netstat -n

Active Connections

Proto	Local Address	Foreign Address	State
TCP	115.246.161.228:3321	209.85.175.125:5222	ESTABLISHED
TCP	115.246.161.228:7850	69.171.228.11:443	ESTABLISHED
TCP	115.246.161.228:7851	124.124.252.64:443	ESTABLISHED
TCP	115.246.161.228:7852	124.124.252.64:443	ESTABLISHED
TCP	115.246.161.228:7853	124.124.252.64:443	ESTABLISHED
TCP	115.246.161.228:7854	124.124.252.64:443	ESTABLISHED
TCP	115.246.161.228:7855	69.171.228.11:443	ESTABLISHED
TCP	115.246.161.228:7862	92.122.126.50:443	ESTABLISHED
TCP	115.246.161.228:7864	124.124.201.160:443	ESTABLISHED
TCP	115.246.161.228:7866	69.171.242.62:443	ESTABLISHED
TCP	115.246.161.228:7869	69.171.228.11:443	ESTABLISHED
TCP	115.246.161.228:7870	124.124.252.64:443	ESTABLISHED
TCP	115.246.161.228:7871	124.124.252.64:443	ESTABLISHED
TCP	115.246.161.228:7872	69.171.227.54:443	ESTABLISHED
TCP	127.0.0.1:31000	127.0.0.1:32000	ESTABLISHED
TCP	127.0.0.1:32000	127.0.0.1:31000	ESTABLISHED

Similarly, there is a very interesting tool called TCP View (can be downloaded for free from www.systeminternals.com) that gives you a list of active processes or applications on your computer and the respective ports and connections that they have currently opened. That also confirms that we are connected to Port 443 (HTTPS) on Facebook:

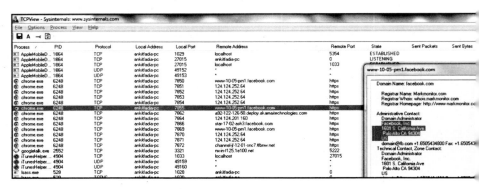

Web Proxy Servers or HTTP Proxy Servers

Usually, whenever we want to visit a website, we start our browser and type the web address of the website that we want to visit in the URL address bar and wait for a response. In the meantime, the browser sends that web address to the local Domain Name Server (DNS) to convert it into its respective IP address. This process of converting a website address or domain name into its respective IP address is known as a DNS lookup. Within a few seconds, your browser will get a response back from the DNS server and will connect you to the respective website.

However, the problem is that nowadays, most colleges, companies and organizations block access to some of the most interesting websites on the Internet by blocking DNS lookups or specific domains. To understand how to unblock access to these blocked websites, it is first important to understand how your local network administrator is blocking access to your favourite websites. Typically, all networks will maintain a database or a list of blocked websites. Whenever you type a website address in your browser, that address is compared with the list of blocked websites. If what you type in your browser is found in the blocked list, your access is blocked and you are shown the ACCESS DENIED error message. On the other hand, if what you type in your browser does not appear in the blocked list, then you will be given access to it.

Let us assume that there is this particular website that you really want to desperately access, but unfortunately your local network administrator has blocked access to it. This is where something known as HTTP proxy server or web proxy server comes into the picture.

A web proxy is a system that is normally accessed by a user with the help of a browser. A web proxy accepts a HTTP request for a specific webpage from a user, processes the request, fetches the required webpage and then displays it immediately back to the user. The firewall or filtering mechanism on the local network of the user thinks that the user is merely connecting to the web proxy (which may not have been blocked), but in reality the user is using the web proxy to connect to some blocked website. In other words, web proxies are fantastic ways to bypass filters and gain access to blocked websites on the Internet.

Web proxy servers not only allow users to bypass blocking censors, but they also protect the IP address or identity of the user giving them complete anonymity on the Internet. Proxy servers act as a mask between you and the Internet hence protecting your identity and giving you anonymity. One of the most popular web proxy servers on the Internet is a website called http://www.anonymizer.com which allows users anonymous access to blocked websites on the Internet. If you connect to their website, this is what you will see on the screen:

Anonymizer.com is a fantastic website and provides an easy, simple-to-use and powerful solution to remaining anonymous while unblocking websites on the Internet. The only problem with the website is that it is not free and will ask you for your credit card information and only once you pay around US$80 will you be allowed to use the service. I am quite sure that everybody reading this book (including me) would rather reveal their identity on the Internet than give their credit card information to this website and pay $80. In fact, I am not even suggesting that you use this website or make any sort of payment to any website.

Instead, all you need to do is start your browser and simply connect to the Russian version of the same website: http://www.anonymizer.ru. As the name suggests, this is a Russian website and there are many practical advantages of using Russian websites. Most of these websites are free (so no credit cards and payments are involved) and more importantly, most of the Russian websites are completely anonymous and do not maintain any records of their users' activities.

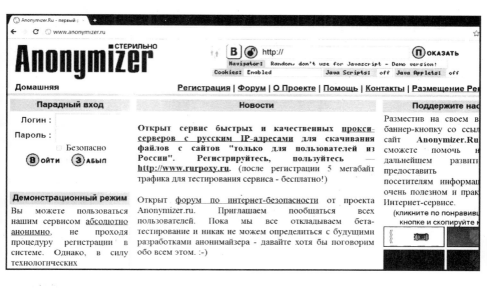

Once you have connected to www.anonymizer.ru then on the right hand side top corner of the screen in the space provided simply type the web address that you wish to visit anonymously and simply click on whatever looks like the SUBMIT button (no need to know how to read Russian!). In this example, I am going to go ahead and type http://www.google.com:

Within a few seconds, www.anonymizer.ru will connect to the Google website, fetch the webpage and display it on your screen. Google will think that somebody from Russia (that is, www.anonymizer.ru) is connecting to it, but in reality, it is you who is hiding behind www.anonymzier.ru and using it to connect to the Google website. As a result, your IP address and identity are completely protected and at the same time, you are able to continue to access your favourite websites on the Internet. Moreover, your local network administrator thinks that you are merely connecting to www.anonymizer.ru and may allow you access to it. Little do they know that you are actually using www.anonymizer.ru to connect to some other blocked websites on the Internet (like the Google website). In the screenshot below you can see how Anonymizer.ru can be used to access the Google website anonymously and safely even if it has been blocked by your network.

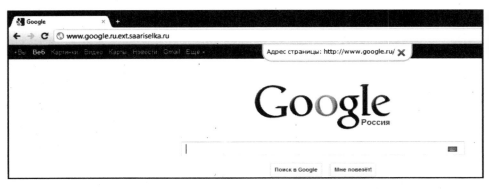

If you look very carefully at the above screenshot, you will notice that everything has been displayed in the Russian language and we are actually connected to the Russian version of Google (that is, www.google.ru). This proves that at this very moment we have successfully managed to fool Google into believing that we are in Russia, even though we are actually still in India. Not only that, we have even fooled our local network and gained access to a blocked website. Just to be 100% sure that www.anonymizer.ru is successfully hiding our IP address and giving us anonymous access to the Internet, we can use our browser to connect to the website www.whatismyipaddress.com.

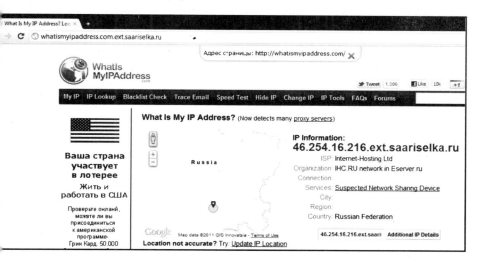

This website reveals that our IP address, network and location have been completely changed and appear to be somewhere in Russia (since we are using the website www.anonymizer.ru). And your local administrator's blocking mechanisms are also bypassed!

To use www.anonymizer.ru you don't always need to go through the entire process of opening the website address in your browser and then typing the requested URL in the appropriate field and then clicking on the submit button. Alternatively, the quicker way of using www.anonymizer.ru is to directly type the following shortcut web address in your web browser:

http://www.domain.com.ext.saariselka.ru/

For example, if you want to anonymously connect to the Google website, then you can directly type the below URL in your browser:

http://www.google.ru.ext.saariselka.ru/

If you use www.anonymizer.com and www.anonymizer.ru long enough then you will realize that sooner or later your network administrator will go ahead and block them as well. But the good news is that there are 1000s of such web proxies available on the Internet. Some of the most popular and reliable ones are the following:

http://www.cooltunnel.com

http://www.bypassthat.com

http://www.btunnel.com

http://ztunnel.com

http://anonymouse.org

http://thexite.com

http://getus.in

http://anonsurf.org

Popular Web Proxies

Below are some of the most popular web-based proxy servers that are currently quite popular and allow users worldwide to access blocked websites on the Internet:

Proxy Server	Website
Aniscartujo	https://aniscartujo.com/webproxy/
	https://aniscartujo.com/ssltunnel/
Free Web Proxy	http://www.free-web-proxy.de/
Dave Proxy	http://daveproxy.co.uk/
Dumb Dream	http://dumbdream.com/
KProxy	http://kproxy.com/
AnonProxy	http://anonproxy.eu/
Try Catch Me	http://www.trycatchme.com/
Poly Solve	http://polysolve.com/links.html
Circumventor	http://peacefire.org/circumventor/
Proxy.org	http://proxy.org/
MegaProxy	https://www.megaproxy.com/freesurf/

16 Glype

In this book we have seen a variety of different proxy servers that can be used to surf the Internet anonymously and unblock access to blocked websites. However, many colleges, companies and organizations are now blocking all the popular proxy servers. In such a scenario, it is possible for users to create and host their own web-based proxy server on the Internet. Glype (http://www.glype.com) is a PHP script that allows you to host your own web-based proxy servers. Since such a web-based proxy server will be hosted on a server of the user's choice, it will be quite difficult for network administrators to block access to them.

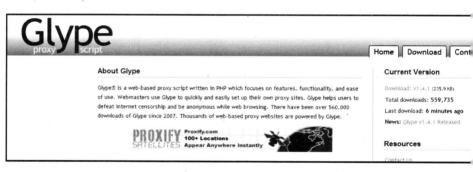

URL Obfuscating
Web Proxies

The problem with the web proxies discussed in the previous section is the fact that the target website address that the user is visiting is revealed within the URL itself and hence this technique can easily be detected and blocked by a network administrator using a URL filtering technique. This is where some URL obfuscating proxies come into the picture. Obfuscation is the technique of hiding a URL address in such a manner that nobody can figure out the actual website address by just looking at it. URL obfuscating proxies do everything that a regular web proxy does, but on top of that they also obfuscate the URL that you are visiting in such a manner that it makes it very tough for the network administrator to be able to detect and block you using URL filtering techniques.

One of my favourite URL obfuscating proxy server is http:// www.hidemyass.com. It allows you to encode a web address in such a manner that nobody can make any sense of it by simply reading or looking at it! All you need to do is connect to this website, type the requested web address in the space provided, select the URL encoding option and then click on the submit button.

If you type www.google.com in the space provided and click on the submit button, then Hide My Ass will obfuscate the web address such that a typical firewall or administrator (that has implemented URL filtering) will not be able to detect what is going on since not only has the URL been encoded, but even the title bar text (that is, Google's home page title bar text) has been removed:

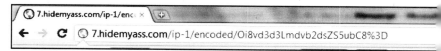

Encoded URLs that are created by Hide My Ass remain the same permanently. In other words, you can bookmark the above mentioned encoded URL and use it at your convenience to access Google through Hide My Ass (http://7.hidemyass.com/ip-1/ encoded/Oi8vd3d3Lmdvb2dsZS5ubC8%3D) by just clicking on your Bookmarks menu.

Encoding is fantastic, but an even better option is the Encryption option available on the Hide My Ass website. The advantage of using the encryption option is that it is a temporary encrypted URL that expires after a set period of time. This means that even in the future, nobody else can view the web pages that may have been visited through it, giving you complete anonymity. Moreover, usually the encryption option carries out on the fly encryption of the URLs, making it a lot harder to block for system administrators:

There are a number of other URL obfuscating proxies that do pretty much the same thing. Some of the most popular ones are listed below:

http://www.blockablock.com/ (Encodes the URL, removes the title bar, HTTPS enabled and accepts cookies)

http://www.airproxy.ca (Encodes the URL, removes the Title Bar, HTTPS enabled and Accepts cookies)

http://www.jellyshell.com/ (Encodes the URL, removes the title bar, HTTPS enabled and accepts cookies)

The Jellyshell website has various mirrors and can also be accessed through http://treesniff.com/, http://headcross.com/ and several other web addresses.

URL obfuscating web proxy servers are very useful. But they could be blocked by your network administrators. In case they block the popular web proxies, then you can always find new web proxies that have not been blocked and continue to access your favourite blocked websites. After a few days, your network administrators will block the new proxies that you are using, then once again you repeat the exercise of finding new web proxies on the Internet. It is an endless cat-and-mouse game!

The problem with web proxies is that you need to always take the trouble of manually connecting to them before you are able to get anonymous unblocked Internet access. It can be quite painful and annoying to do that manually every single time we want to access a blocked website. Wouldn't it be fantastic if there was a way to configure your browser to automatically connect to a proxy server and give us anonymous unrestricted access to the Internet?

It is important to note that if you want to log into any of your online accounts (like Facebook, Gmail, Yahoo or Hotmail), you will need to find and use a web proxy that accepts cookies. Another problem with web proxies is that many of them do not support JavaScript and SSL encryption, which means that a number of websites will not work. For example, you may not be allowed to watch streaming videos on YouTube if scripts are not supported by your proxy.

⬡ 18   Proxy Lists

Web proxies are very useful. But the problem with web proxies is the fact that you need to manually type the address of the web proxy in your browser and then use it to connect to the website that you wish to unblock. Imagine doing this every single time you start your browser. That can be quite inconvenient and slow. It is possible to configure your browser to automatically connect to a proxy server without you having to do anything manually:

STEP 1: There are various websites on the Internet that publish a list of hundreds of different proxy servers from different parts of the world. One of my personal favourite such proxy list website is http://www.samair.ru/proxy which at any given point of time can have anywhere between a few hundred to a few thousand different proxy servers listed on it. At the time of writing, this website had 1381 different proxy servers available on it. You can use any of these 1381 proxy servers to bypass the filtering mechanism or firewall of your college or company and continue to access any of your favourite blocked websites on the Internet. If your local network wants to block you, they will have to manually block all the 1381 proxy servers listed on this website one by one, which is quite a herculean task. Even if they manage to block each and every one of these 1381 different proxy servers, the best part about this website is the fact that this list of proxy servers is updated every hour, with new proxy servers being constantly added to it. This means that you can always come back in an hour and get access to new proxy servers that have been added to the list. So never ever get blocked again!

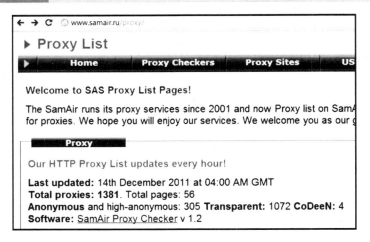

STEP 2: From the list of proxy servers, select any that you wish to connect. I want to pretend to be in Argentina so am going to select the proxy server below:

Proxy IP address: 201.216.234.9

Proxy Port: 8080

Proxy Location: Argentina

Most of the proxy servers that you will find in online lists will be running on either of the below ports:

Port Number	Function
80	Default port for all HTTP-related access. Almost all websites are hosted on Port 80 of a server.
8080	Port has traditionally been the alternative to Port 80.
3128	Commonly used proxy port

It is a common practice for system administrators to block outgoing connections to Port 8080 and 3128 to prevent the use of proxy servers. However, no system administrator can block outgoing connections to Port 80, since that would prevent users from accessing even regular websites!

190.210.94.89:8081	transparent proxy	135 minutes ago	Argentina
190.245.190.67:8080	transparent proxy	135 minutes ago	Argentina
186.153.144.10:8080	transparent	138 minutes ago	Argentina
190.3.106.166:80	high-anonymous server	102 minutes ago	Argentina
186.153.121.18:8080	transparent proxy	101 minutes ago	Argentina
190.226.225.16:8080	transparent	135 minutes ago	Argentina
186.109.89.208:3128	transparent proxy	138 minutes ago	Argentina
201.216.234.9:8080	anonymous proxy server	99 minutes ago	Argentina
190.16.117.200:8080	transparent server	136 minutes ago	Argentina
190.18.236.233:8080	transparent proxy	136 minutes ago	Argentina
190.229.128.30:3128	transparent	119 minutes ago	Argentina
186.129.253.214:8080	transparent proxy	138 minutes ago	Argentina
190.189.90.189:8080	transparent proxy	136 minutes ago	Argentina

STEP 3: Once you have selected which proxy server you wish to connect to, you need to start your browser and configure it to connect to the proxy server. I am going to use Internet Explorer in this example, but the same process can be used on all popular browsers. Click on TOOLS >INTERNET OPTIONS > Connections Tab >SETTINGS button, enable the use of a Proxy Server option, type the address 201.216.234.9 and Port 8080 and click on OK to save the settings . You may have to restart your browser on certain occasions.

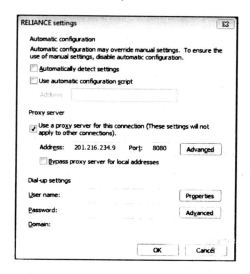

STEP 4: To test whether the proxy server is configured properly and is giving you anonymous unblocked access to the Internet, just point your browser to http://www.whatismyipaddress.com, and you will notice that your IP address has now changed to the IP address of the proxy server (201.216.234.9) and your location has been changed to Buenos Aires in Argentina. In reality, I am still sitting here in Mumbai, India. Your local network will think that you are connecting to a random server in Argentina, hence will not block you. But in reality you are using this Argentinian proxy server to connect to blocked websites.

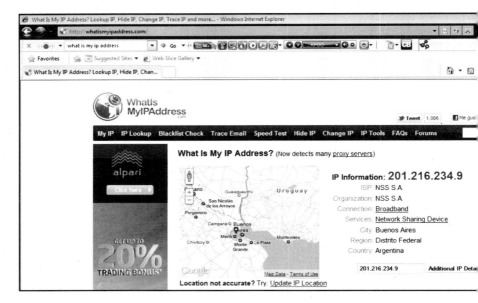

STEP 5: Let us assume after some time you get bored or want to now pretend to be in some other part of the world, say, Thailand. You can go back to the proxy list available on http://www.samair.ru/proxy and select a proxy server which is located in any country of your choice (in this case Thailand). I am now going to configure my browser to connect to the proxy server 203.158.192.10 running on Port 8080 and located in Thailand and my identity would change!

IP address	Anonymity level	Checked time	Country
118.175.14.50:3128	high-anonymous proxy server	150 minutes ago	Thailand
110.77.234.72:3128	transparent proxy	167 minutes ago	Thailand
61.19.127.131:8080	anonymous server	159 minutes ago	Thailand
203.113.116.115:8080	transparent proxy server	165 minutes ago	Thailand
202.60.204.14:8080	transparent proxy	165 minutes ago	Thailand
61.19.236.213:80	transparent proxy	166 minutes ago	Thailand
27.131.130.66:8080	transparent proxy	167 minutes ago	Thailand
203.158.192.10:8080	high-anonymous proxy server	163 minutes ago	Thailand
Fast Anonymous Proxy			
61.7.241.18:3128	transparent	168 minutes ago	Thailand
203.28.128.22:3128	transparent proxy	171 minutes ago	Thailand

STEP 6: It is possible to configure absolutely any browser to connect through a proxy server of your choice. In the previous example, we had played with Internet Explorer. Now, let us do the same on my favourite browser Google Chrome. You have click on the TOOLS WRENCH button > Options > Under the Hood > Change Proxy Settings > Settings button > Enable the Use Proxy server option and enter the proxy server 203.158.192.10 and Port 8080. Now, Google Chrome is also configured to connect through the proxy server.

STEP 7: Once again, a quick test using http://www.whatismyipaddress.com reveals that we have successfully managed to change our identity and location within a matter of a few minutes! Now you can appear to be located in Thailand.

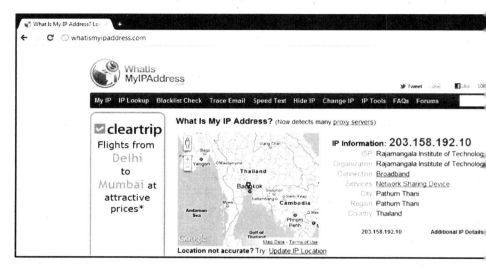

After configuring your browser to use a proxy server in this manner, if you were to go to the MSDOS prompt and type the *netstat –n* command then you will notice that the browser is routing all outgoing connections via Port 8080 (see highlighted below) on the remote proxy server that we had selected:

C:\Users\ankitfadia>netstat -n

Active Connections

Proto	Local Address	Foreign Address	State
TCP	115.246.197.16:5539	209.85.175 125:5222	ESTABLISHED
TCP	115.246.197.16:5700	203.158.192.10:8080	ESTABLISHED
TCP	115.246.197.16:5705	203.158 192.10:8080	ESTABLISHED
TCP	115.246.197.16:5706	203.158.192.10:8080	ESTABLISHED
TCP	115.246.197.16:5752	203.158 192.10:8080	ESTABLISHED

TCP	115.246.197.16:5753	203.158.192.10:8080	ESTABLISHED
TCP	115.246.197.16:5776	203.158.192.10:8080	ESTABLISHED
TCP	115.246.197.16:5777	203.158.192.10:8080	ESTABLISHED
TCP	115.246.197.16:5786	203.158.192.10:8080	ESTABLISHED
TCP	115.246.197.16:5787	203.158.192.10:8080	ESTABLISHED
TCP	115.246.197.16:5788	203.158.192.10:8080	ESTABLISHED
TCP	115.246.197.16:5789	203.158.192.10:8080	ESTABLISHED
TCP	115.246.197.16:5792	203.158.192.10:8080	ESTABLISHED
TCP	115.246.197.16:5794	203.158.192.10:8080	ESTABLISHED
TCP	115.246.197.16:5795	203.158.192.10:8080	ESTABLISHED
TCP	127.0.0.1:1029	127.0.0.1:5354	ESTABLISHED
TCP	127.0.0.1:1032	127.0.0.1:27015	ESTABLISHED
TCP	127.0.0.1:5354	127.0.0.1:1029	ESTABLISHED
TCP	127.0.0.1:27015	127.0.0.1:1032	ESTABLISHED

One of the biggest advantages of connecting to a proxy server by configuring your browser instead of using web proxies is that they are usually cookies and scripting enabled. This means that you can use these proxy servers and still be able to log into your online accounts and even stream videos off the Internet. There are numerous websites that publish proxy server lists. Some of the most popular ones are the following:

http://www.hidemyass.com/proxy-list/

ast update	IP address	Port	Country	Speed	Connection time	Type	Anonymity
7 secs	81.89.59.206	8080	Slovakia			HTTPS	High +KA
7 secs	87.106.143.132	3128	Germany			HTTPS	High +KA
7 secs	178.168.28.195	8080	Moldova, Republic of			HTTPS	High +KA
7 secs	93.157.254.37	8080	Russian Federation			HTTPS	High +KA
7 secs	118.97.193.202	3128	Indonesia			HTTPS	High +KA
7 secs	194.170.16.75	8088	United Arab Emirates			HTTPS	High +KA
7 secs	159.148.213.227	3128	Latvia			HTTPS	High +KA
7 secs	188.93.20.179	8080	Russian Federation			HTTP	Medium
7 secs	201.73.83.130	3128	Brazil			HTTPS	High +KA

http://xroxy.com/

http://www.proxy.org

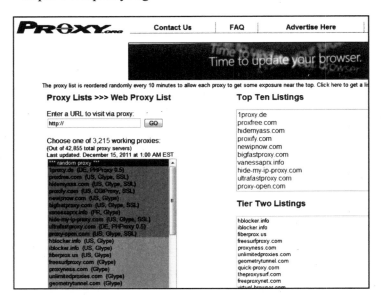

http://multiproxy.org

```
75.94.67.90:1080
201.26.8.186:1080
201.93.128.110:1080
202.57.10.25:1080
201.90.55.194:1080
217.219.80.3:1080
218.241.238.141:1080
202.98.141.200:1080
68.20.20.140:6475
218.56.21.226:1080
213.255.196.219:1080
218.64.215.86:1080
219.150.227.101:1080
219.159.199.34:1080
222.134.69.181:8000
222.188.10.1:1080
68.82.102.9:25552
80.108.206.239:11033
85.113.252.214:1080
86.100.64.151:14841
85.132.201.196:25552
82.228.53.39:11033
80.35.156.3:17327
82.238.32.72:14848
89.77.158.227:17327
87.97.237.135:11033
69.226.246.172:41941
89.77.94.73:22568
69.116.194.146:3073
83.143.145.67:1080
88.174.252.233:11011
71.145.167.207:15621
```

Total: 1527 proxy servers found.

19

Proxy Bouncing or
Proxy Chains

In the previous sections, we have already seen how it is possible to connect to a proxy server to bypass the local filtering mechanism and hide your identity on the Internet. Proxy Servers act as a mask between you and the Internet and thus protect your identity and give you anonymity on the Internet. Proxy Servers are great. But if you are really paranoid about your revealing your identity and want to add multiple layers of security and anonymity to your online presence, there is a very interesting technique known as Proxy Bouncing.

Proxy Bouncing is the art of connecting to multiple proxy servers one after the other to form a proxy chain. Each proxy server in a proxy chain provides additional security and anonymity to the user, making it harder for the user to be traced back. Once the proxy chain has been established, all data communication that the user carries out can be configured to pass through it. This technique of proxy bouncing can not only be used to bypass blocking mechanisms implemented by the network administrator, but can also be used to remain completely anonymous and secure on the Internet.

SocksChain (http://ufasoft.com/socks/) is a useful tool that allows users to establish a chain of proxy servers on the Internet. Most applications can be configured to connect to the proxy chain created by SocksChain for anonymous secure communication on the Internet.

As soon as you start SocksChain, it will connect to its directory server to download a list of available proxy servers. It will then open Port 1081 on the local system and will listen for any incoming connections. Let us assume that you want to use Google Chrome to connect to the Internet after performing proxy bouncing via SocksChain. To do that, you need to start Google Chrome and change the proxy settings such that it will connect to the SocksChain proxy on the location system 127.0.0.1 on Port 1081. Similarly you can configure other applications on your computer to connect to the Internet through SocksChain by changing the proxy settings.

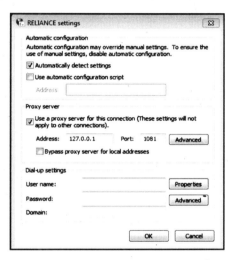

I have configured both Internet Explorer and Google Chrome to connect to SocksChain on Port 1081 and as soon as I start the two browsers, the SocksChain software starts creating the proxy chain:

```
ocksChain
View  Tools  Help
  firefox
  chrome
    Through $50DD343021E509EB3A5A7FD0D8A4F8364AFBDCB5=venus, $9F89491CAB7B03685DEABD358E193FFA74D8D836=BigBoy, $57E4CC538020E1F7A04D40124B21590D1B7A66A8~tgen2
      To plus.google.com[173.194.70.100]:443  3 connections
      To plusone.google.com[74.125.224.98]:443  3 connections
      To www.facebook.com[69.171.224.11]:443  3 connections
      To www.google-analytics.com[173.194.70.101]:80  1 connections
      To pubads.g.doubleclick.net[173.194.70.155]:80  1 connections
      To www.facebook.com[69.171.224.11]:80  1 connections
      To redirect.sockschain.com[69.73.179.91]:80  18 connections
  iexplore
    Through $50DD343021E509EB3A5A7FD0D8A4F8364AFBDCB5=venus, $9F89491CAB7B03685DEABD358E193FFA74D8D836=BigBoy, $57E4CC538020E1F7A04D40124B21590D1B7A66A8~tgen2
      To www.google.com[74.125.224.115]:80  2 connections
```

To check whether the proxy chain has been established or not, we can connect the browsers to the website http://www.whatismyipaddress.com:

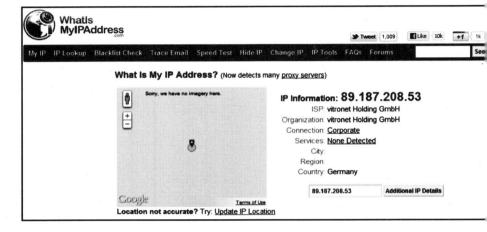

Public DNS Systems

A DNS (Domain Name Server) lookup is a query sent by a user (browser, IM or email client) to a DNS server to convert a particular domain name into its respective IP address. Many organizations and colleges have a habit of blocking access to certain websites by either blocking DNS queries to those domain names or by redirecting users requesting that domain name to an internal 'This website is blocked' page. For example, whenever you type www.facebook.com in your browser, your browser sends a DNS request to the local network's DNS server, which could block the user or redirect the user to some other website. In the previous sections we have already seen how to circumvent the local DNS server of your company or college by typing the IP addresses in various formats instead of typing the domain name of the website that you want to visit. However, in case your organization has blocked by IP address, then you will not be able to access the requested website.

It is possible for a user to bypass such a blocking mechanism by using public DNS servers instead of the local DNS servers in their network. Some of the most popular public DNS servers are OpenDNS (http://www.opendns.com/), Google DNS (http://code.google.com/speed/public-dns/), DNS Advantage (http://www.dnsadvantage.com/), Visizone DNS (http://visizone.com/), Norton DNS (https://dns.norton.com) and DNS Resolvers (http://dnsresolvers.com/). Your local DNS server will normally block all the interesting websites on the Internet that you wish to access. On the other hand, public DNS servers will not block any legal website like YouTube, Facebook, Orkut and others. Hence, by not using the local DNS servers and replacing them with public DNS servers, it is possible for users to bypass any DNS blocking mechanisms that may be in place.

Normally, whenever you connect to a network like your company, college or ISP, then your computer automatically obtains the DNS server address that it needs to connect to, which usually belongs to and is controlled by your network provider. Sometimes, your network provider will require you to manually enter the DNS server addresses on your computer. Either way, since you will be going through a DNS server that is controlled and managed by your network provider, you will not be able to access websites that they don't want you to access. This is where public DNS servers are so useful.

I am a big Google products lover and it is obvious that my favourite public DNS system is the Google Public DNS system (http://code.google.com/speed/public-dns/). In this section, we will see an example of how to use the Google Public DNS system to unblock websites on the Internet. All other public DNS systems are similar in nature and can be configured in a similar manner. The Google Public DNS server addresses are the following:

- 8.8.8.8
- 8.8.4.4

To make your computer connect to the Google Public DNS system, you will have to follow the below steps:

STEP 1: Open CONTROL PANEL > NETWORK AND INTERNET > NETWORK AND SHARING CENTER and then click on CHANGE ADAPTER SETTINGS.

STEP 2: Right click on the Connection that you want to configure to use the Google Public DNS system, click on Properties and then click on the Networking tab.

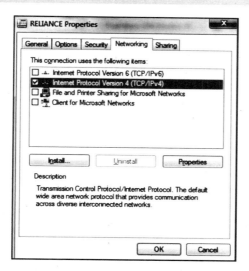

STEP 3: Select the Internet Protocol Version 4 option and click on the PROPERTIES button and under the GENERAL tab, select the option USE THE FOLLOWING DNS SERVER ADDRESSES and enter the Google DNS server addresses: 8.8.8.8 and 8.8.4.4.

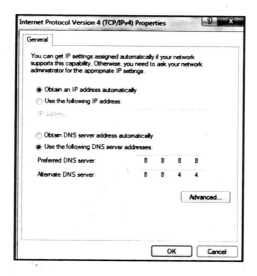

STEP 4: Disconnect from the network and reconnect. Your connection is now configured to connect to the Google Public DNS servers. Now you can enjoy a fully unblocked Internet without any DNS filtering in place.

Other than unblocking websites, there are many other advantages of using such public DNS servers instead of the local DNS servers:

- Usually faster due to server locations + large cached databases.

- Corrects typos (gogle.com automatically becomes google.com)

- Includes filtering and protection against phishing.

- Uses shortcuts instead of complete domain names.

Some of the other popular public DNS systems and their respective DNS server addresses are listed below:

Public DNS System	DNS Servers	
Google DNS	8.8.8.8	8.8.4.4
Open DNS	208.67.222.222	208.67.220.220
DNS Advantage	156.154.70.1	156.154.71.1
VisiZone	74.50.55.161	74.50.55.162
Norton DNS	198.153.192.1	198.153.194.1
DNS Resolvers	205.210.42.205	64.68.200.200

Ultrasurf

Ultrasurf is one of my favourite anti-censorship and anti-blocking software on the Internet. It is free, fast and really effective. Ultrasurf was originally created by the Ultrareach Internet Corporation to help Internet users in China to bypass filtering and censorship by the government. However, now Ultrasurf is amongst the most popular unblocking tools available on the Internet. It is available as a free download at http://ultrasurf.us/index.html. Unlike traditional proxy servers, Ultrasurf supports cookies, scripts and even SSL!

The best part about Ultrasurf is that it does not require any installation or configuration. It is just a little more than a 1 MB download, which can be carried around by you in a USB pen drive, MP3 player or the micro SD card of your camera to office or college. It is possible to simply double click on the Ultrasurf EXE file and immediately get unblocked and unrestricted access to the Internet. You can access even blocked stuff on the Internet using Ultrasurf. No installation, no registration, no hassles! Sometimes, system administrators will try to prevent users from using Ultrasurf by blocking its process name from being allowed to be loaded into the memory or being executed. In such a case, it is possible for users to simply rename the name of the EXE file to anything of their choice and continue using it! For example, in the screenshot below, the Ultrasurf EXE file has been renamed to Ankit Fadia and it still works:

library ▼ Share with ▼ New folder			
Name	Date modified	Type	Size
utmp	13-12-2011 16:36	File folder	
Ankit Fadia	13-12-2011 15:52	Application	1,220 KB
u	13-12-2011 16:33	Configuration sett...	1 KB

Even in the Task Manager (Ctrl + Alt + Del) the name of the process in the memory has been changed, hence allowing a user to fool any application or process blocking that might have been implemented by the local system administrator to prevent the use of Ultrasurf:

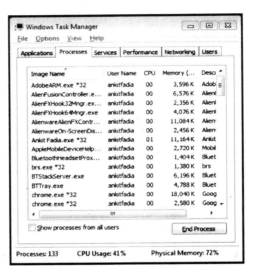

Once you have disguised the file name of the Ultrasurf Application (which was an optional step), you can start using Ultrasurf by following the simple steps below:

STEP 1: Before we start Ultrasurf, let us quickly check the current actual IP address of my system by opening my browser and connecting to the website http://www.whatismyipaddress. com. Within a few seconds it tells us that my IP address is 115.246.15.116, my current ISP is Reliance Communications and location is New Delhi, India. We will test my IP address and location again after running Ultrasurf.

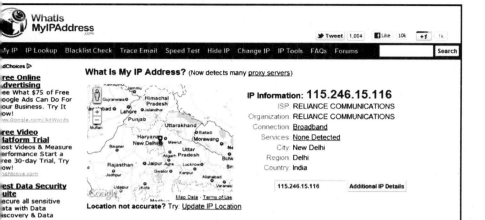

STEP 2: Double click on the Ultrasurf EXE file and it should automatically open the console window shown below. Ultrasurf will first automatically connect to its central server (which has a long database of available proxy servers) and find the best available proxy server and then establish a secure connection with it. Once the secure anonymous connection with the proxy has been established, Ultrasurf will automatically open an Internet Explorer window. Typically, there will be a golden coloured padlock on the right bottom corner of the browser window signifying that a secure connection has been established. If you want to change your identity at any point or want to change your connection route, then you can do that from this console window itself by clicking on the check boxes:

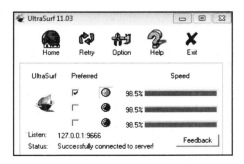

STEP 3: To test whether your connection is truly anonymous, connect to the website www.whatismyipaddress. com. Based on the screenshot below, my IP address has been suddenly changed to 65.49.14.86 and my location is not showing anymore. If you look very carefully, then you will notice that on the graphical user interface map, my location is coming up as being in the middle of the ocean off the coast of Africa. There is no island there, but the server has been configured in such a manner so as to show such a cool location!

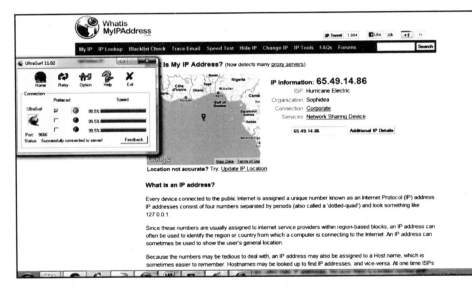

STEP 4: By default when you start Ultrasurf, it will only allow you to use the Internet Explorer browser to establish secure anonymous connections. What do you do if you want to configure other browsers and applications to also use Ultrasurf for secure anonymous Internet access? For example, let us assume that you want to configure the Google Chrome browser to connect to the Internet via the Ultrasurf browser – all you need to do is start Google Chrome and click on TOOLS Wrench Button > Options > Under the Hood > Change Proxy Settings >Lan Settings. Now enable the Use Proxy Server option and enter 127.0.0.1 (this is the

loopback IP address that represents the local system) in the Address field and 9666 in the Port field. Port 9666 on your local machine is the port where Ultrasurf is listening for any incoming connections, hence allowing even your Google Chrome browser to now be configured to connect to the Internet via Ultrasurf.

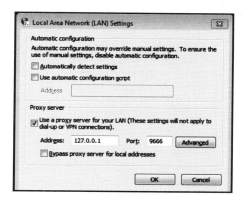

To test if Google Chrome has been configured properly, simply connect to www.whatismyipaddress.com and you will notice the same IP address and location that was showing up in the Internet Explorer window earlier.

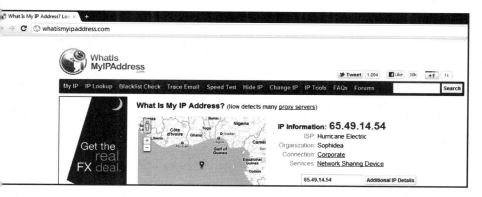

Ultrasurf by default listens for connections on local Port 9666, which means that they can blocked by system administrators by blocking traffic to Port 9666. To make it harder for system administrators to detect and filter the use of Ultrasurf, it is possible to change the default port being used by it. All you have to do is start Ultrasurf and then click on OPTIONS and then change the Local Listening Port value to any value of your choice:

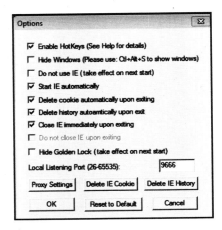

The best feature about Ultrasurf is that when you close it, it will automatically delete all entries from the browsing history and cookies on your system, leaving absolutely no trace behind.

22   Your Freedom

Normally, your computer directly connects to the Internet, hence your identity is revealed to everybody on the Internet. Moreover, any websites that are blocked by your local system administrator cannot be accessed by you. This is where *Your Freedom* comes into the picture. It is a proxy software that can be installed on your computer. Once installed, all applications on your computer can connect to one of the proxy servers of *Your Freedom* and disguise your identity. Not only that, *Your Freedom,* through its proxies, allows users to connect to blocked websites on the Internet.

Your Freedom is available as a free download on the Internet on its website http://www.your-freedom.net. However, in case your system administrator has blocked access to this website, then there are multiple mirrors which can be used to download it. It is also possible to download it via email.

In order to start using the *Your Freedom* software, you must register on its website and create an account for yourself. However, the good news is that the installation and registration process is quite simple and straightforward. The basic version of *Your Freedom* is free, while the premium version is not free but gives users higher bandwidth. Once the software is installed on your computer, it will start a configuration wizard which guides you through the process of preparing your system to connect to the *Your Freedom* network.

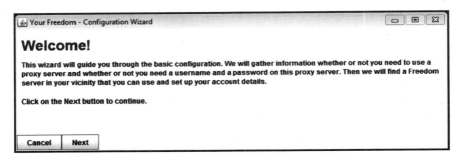

Just follow the instructions displayed by the configuration wizard and soon *Your Freedom* will connect to its central database and will download a list of proxy servers and test them:

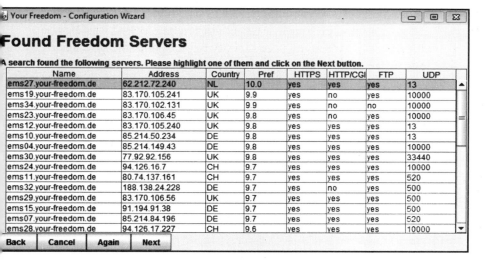

As a final step, *Your Freedom* will ask you to enter your username and password and once you login you are ready to start unblocking websites on the Internet. Please note that you will have to manually configure your browser and other applications to connect to *Your Freedom* on Port 8080 (Web Proxy) or Port 1080 (SOCKS proxy) for the connection to work properly.

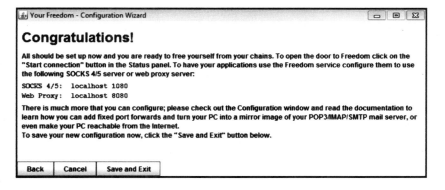

Now *Your Freedom* has been successfully set up and installed on your computer. You will be able to access blocked websites on the Internet. Moreover, your identity will be complete safe, secure and anonymous.

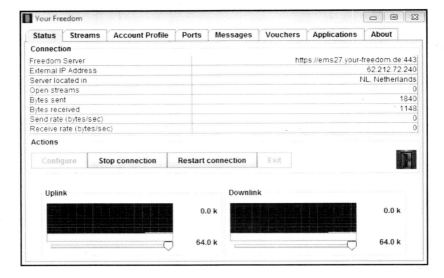

23 The Onion Router (TOR)

Tor stands for the Onion Router and is a free software that is one of the best anonymity, privacy and unblocking tools available on the Internet. Tor has thousands of volunteer relay servers in different parts of the world through which a user's data is routed and tunnelled in encrypted format with the intention of keeping it completely anonymous. Not only does it protect your freedom on the Internet by allowing you to access all your favourite websites on the Internet, it keeps all your communications on the Internet completely secure. It can be downloaded free of cost from https://www.torproject.org.

A number of organizations and governments like to monitor the Internet by performing something known as traffic analysis. For example, imagine your company could be running a data sniffer on the company network to look at the traffic on the network to figure out what websites and servers employees are accessing. At a bigger level, the government could be running a data sniffer on all the major ISPs' networks with the intention to record, monitor and analyse traffic of all users in a country. This information could then be used to block access to certain websites as well.

Typically, all data is being transmitted on the Internet in the form of data packets. Each data packet has two parts:

- **Data:** This is the actual data that is being transmitted in the data packet. It could be a part of an email, file or web page.

- **Header:** This contains important information about the source and destination computers that is used to route the data through the Internet.

There are a lot of ways in which the data being transmitted on the Internet can be encrypted. For example, it is possible to encrypt an email using PGP encryption and then send it out on the Internet. However, encrypting the actual data does not hide the header of a data packet. This means that somebody who is using a data sniffer at your ISP or company or college network could still easily read the header part of the data transfer and figure out valuable information about the source and destination of the data packets. For every data communication on the Internet, there are multiple such intermediaries that could be monitoring and spying on your data communication like your college, company, ISP or even the government. In other words, imagine that you want to communicate with your bank, then typically something like the following communication route is established:

YOUR COMPUTER → COMPANY or COLLEGE network → ISP Network → ISP Backbone → Bank's ISP → BANK

Obviously, in a communication like the above, your computer and your bank will know everything about both the data and the data header. But based on how Internet routing works, all intermediaries along the way (like your company/college, ISP, ISP backbone, Bank's ISP and others) could be spying upon the data header and even the data (if it is not encrypted) using a simple data sniffer. This means that the source and destination computers have no anonymity on the Internet. All intermediaries know who the source and the destination are.

One of my personal favourite data sniffers is a free software called Wireshark (http://www.wireshark.org/) that allows criminal or system administrators to monitor all data packets being sent and received across the entire network. Even if a user has encrypted the actual data being sent on the Internet, Wireshark can be used to record and analyse the header information to figure out valuable details about the source and destination involved in the data transfer.

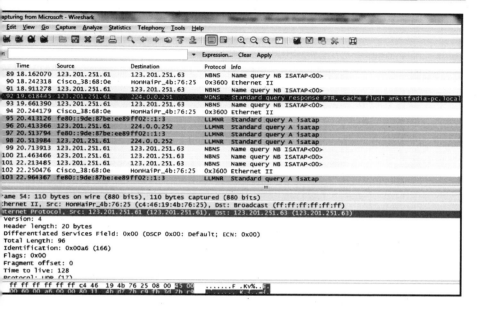

This is where Onion Routing comes into the picture. It is an anonymous communication mechanism that ensures that the intermediaries can read neither the data nor the data header that they are transmitting, hence giving complete anonymity to both the sender and the destination systems.

Typically in onion routing, the entire data is repeatedly encrypted with multiple layers of encryption (just the way an onion has multiple layers of skin) and these encryption layers are slowly peeled until the data reaches the destination computer. Once data is encrypted at the source computer it is then routed through multiple intermediate nodes called onion routers. Whenever data reaches an onion router, it will peel a layer of encryption to reveal information about the next onion router node to which the data has to be forwarded. The next onion router will repeat the procedure and peel the next layer of encryption, forward the data again and so on. This process is repeated until all the encryption layers are peeled and the data reaches the destination computer. Such a multilayered encryption and routing mechanism ensures that none of the intermediaries know anything about the contents of the data, the source or the destination. The best part is that no intermediary onion router knows the complete path. Each intermediary onion router will only know where it got the data from and the next system it is supposed to send the data to. The destination system (recipient of the data) will think that all the data originated at the last onion router and not the source system.

Tor is a fantastic free utility that uses Onion Routing to provide users with a secure, anonymous and encrypted communication channel for all their data transfer needs. Once installed, all applications on your computer can be configured to communicate on the Internet through the Tor relay servers (onion routers) in different parts of the world. According to the Tor project's website (http://www.torproject.org), Tor works in the following steps:

STEP 1: Let us assume that you want to connect to www.domain.comthrough an encrypted communication channel that is completely secure and anonymous at the same time. You need to install Tor on your computer and make sure that you have configured your browser to connect to the Internet through Tor. (We will see how to do that later on in this book.) Once Tor receives your request to connect to www.domain.com, it will first connect to the Tor directory server and download a list of all available Tor relay nodes (onion routers) that it can potentially connect to.

STEP 2: Tor will now create a secure encrypted connection between you and www.domain.com by routing the connection through any three randomly selected Tor relay nodes (onion routers) one after the other. This path that Tor creates is known as a Tor circuit. Tor will make use of Onion Routing principals while establishing this encrypted secure Tor circuit. Tor always connects to a minimum of three randomly selected Tor relay routers in any part of the world before connecting the user to the destination system, hence ensuring adequately randomized anonymity. The advantage of Tor over a proxy server is that Tor ensures that you are always routed via a minimum of three different Tor relay servers. On the other hand, in case of a proxy server, you are normally routed only through one system.

STEP 3: Once a Tor circuit has been created, it will continue to be used for all connections for 10 minutes or so, after which all new connections will be given completely new Tor circuits. It is also possible to force Tor to change its circuit sooner than 10 minutes if required. Whenever Tor changes its circuit, your identity on the Internet also changes.

Now that we have understood how Tor circuits are established and how Tor works, let us now put this knowledge to use and actually use it to anonymously and safely unblock a blocked website on the Internet.

STEP 1: Download the Tor Browser Bundle, which is available as a free download on the tor website https://www.torproject.org. The Tor Browser Bundle is a self-contained executable file that can be run directly from a USB pen drive or even a camera SD Card without the need for any installation or configuration. It comes with a copy of the Firefox Portable browser preconfigured and allows users to establish a secure encrypted connection easily and quickly without any hassle of configuration.

STEP 2: After downloading the Tor Browser Bundle, you need to extract it to a folder of your choice. It could be anywhere on

your hard drive or even on an external USB pen drive. To launch Tor, you just need to go to the respective folder and double click on the *Start Tor Browser* icon.

Start Tor Browser   FirefoxPortable   Docs   Data   App

STEP 3: As soon as you double click on the *Start Tor Browser* icon, the Vidalia Control Panel will open. At this stage, Tor will connect to its directory server and download a list of available Tor relay servers (onion routers) and then try to establish a secure encrypted Tor circuit through any three different randomly selected Tor relay servers. This entire process of establishing a Tor circuit should not take more than a few seconds. As soon as a secure Tor circuit has been established, a new Mozilla Firefox browser window will automatically open.

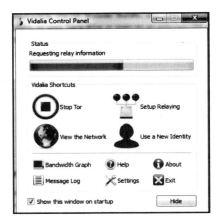

Once Mozilla Firefox launches, it means that the secure Tor circuit has been established and you can start browsing the Internet securely and anonymously. The Firefox Mozilla window that opens will also say *Congratulations. Your Browser is configured to use Tor,* letting you know that Tor is now ready to be used.

STEP 4: Let us quickly test the Tor circuit by opening the website www.whatismyipaddress.com to check if our connection is anonymous or not. In this case if you look at the screenshot below, you will notice that Tor has routed our connection through a Germany-based relay server whose IP address is 87.78.51.16.

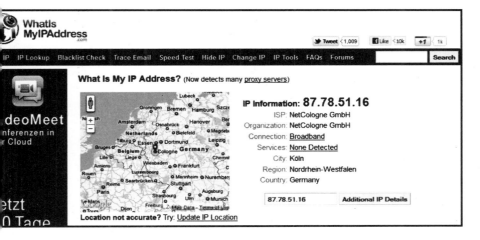

It is important to note that the Tor browser bundle only works with the Portable Firefox Browser that it automatically opens once the Tor circuit gets established. All other applications, including other browsers installed on your system, will not automatically start connecting to the Tor circuit. For example, if you simultaneously open both Google Chrome and Mozilla Firefox portable browser to http://www.whatismyipaddress.com, then you will get two different IP addresses and two different locations in two different browsers at the same time!

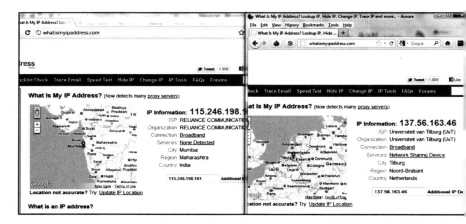

Let us assume that after some time you get bored of being in Germany and want to reroute your secure tor circuit through some other country. All you need to do is in the Vidalia Control Panel you need to click on the *Use a New Identity* option and within a few seconds Tor will create a brand new Tor circuit for you, giving you a completely new location and IP address:.

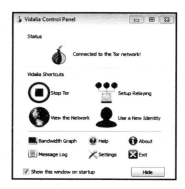

Now if you were to open www.whatismyipaddress.com in the Mozilla Firefox browser, then you will notice that you IP address has changed to 137.56.163.46 and your location to the Netherlands!

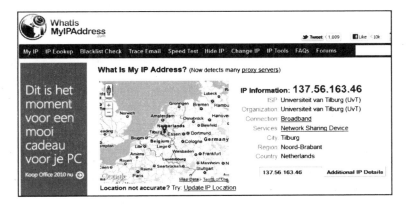

Typically at any given point of time, Tor will have a few thousand different volunteer tor servers/onion routers (at the time of writing this book 2,337 relay servers were online) in different parts of the world. It is possible for a user to view all the tor relay servers online at any given point of time by opening the Vidalia Control Panel and clicking on the View the Network link to display the Tor Network Map:

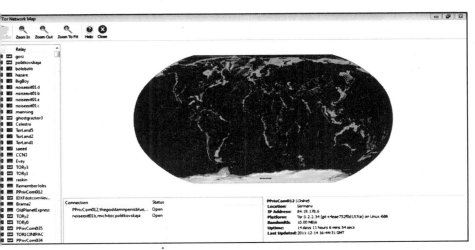

Within this Tor Network Map window, in the right bottom pane, information about all the three Tor relay servers through which your computer has currently established a circuit is available. Currently my computer's Tor circuit is as follows:

Computer → Tor Relay Server 1 in the United States → Tor Relay Server 2 in the Netherlands → Tor Relay Server 3 in the Netherlands → Internet

Amunet3 (Online)
Location: United States
IP Address: 199.48.147.37
Platform: Tor 0.2.2.34 (git-f0e1ee98af443107) on Linux x86_64
Bandwidth: 6.84 MB/s
Uptime: 47 days 17 hours 39 mins 42 secs
Last Updated: 2011-12-14 08:58:52 GMT

KpnFiberTest (Online)
Location: Netherlands
IP Address: 145.53.65.130
Platform: Tor 0.2.2.34 (git-c4eae752f0d157ce) on Linux x86_64
Bandwidth: 3.47 MB/s
Uptime: 11 days 14 hours 21 mins 3 secs
Last Updated: 2011-12-14 08:01:17 GMT

TORy1 (Online)
Location: Netherlands
IP Address: 137.56.163.64
Platform: Tor 0.2.3.7-alpha (git-a1a44384422174d9) on Linux x86_64
Bandwidth: 10.74 MB/s
Uptime: 27 days 15 hours 50 mins 55 secs
Last Updated: 2011-12-14 13:05:24 GMT

Sometimes, your company, college or government will block access to the Tor project website trying to prevent users from being able to download and use Tor. The good news is that it is possible to download Tor through email as well! Just send an email to gettor@torproject.org from any email account that can accept large attachments (like Gmail or Yahoo). Make sure you type *help* in the body of the email and they will get back to you with instructions ón how to download a relevant Tor package via email:

As described in their instructions email, if you want to receive the Tor Browser Bundle for Windows, you need to send an email to them at gettor@torproject.org with the keyword *windows* in the body of the email. Within a few seconds they will send you a detailed email with the Tor Browser Bundle for Windows attached. As simple as that!

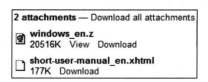

How to Unblock Websites and Surf Anonymously using your Android Phone

In the previous section, we saw how easy it is to use Tor to surf the Internet anonymously and unblock blocked websites using your computer. However, what happens if instead of using a desktop, you are using a mobile phone to access the Internet. If you are worried that your government or company is monitoring your mobile activity or if you wish to unblock access to your favourite blocked websites on your mobile phone, then Orbot can be extremely useful. It is an open source client for Android phones, that allows you to connect to the tor network and route all your traffic from mobile applications (like browser, email client, instant messenger etc) through tor anonymously and securely. Orbot is presently pretty much the only app available to Android users who wish to connect to tor. Imagine all the benefits of tor, but on your Android phone!

It is possible to download and install the Orbotapp from the Official Android Marketplace or by connecting the browser on your Android phone to the official Tor project websitehttps:// www.torproject.org and downloading the Tor Android Bundle.

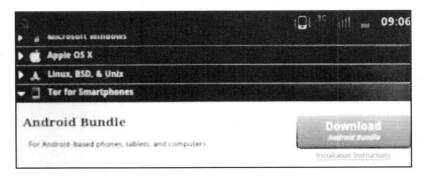

The process of installing Tor is extremely easy and you just need to follow the instructions that display on your mobile phone screen. However, just installing Orbot, does not allow you to surf the Internet anonymously. You also need to install a compatible browser which can work with the Tor project. The good news is that during installation of the Tor Android Bundle itself, you will be prompted to download the Orweb browser that is designed to work with the Tor software. It is highly recommended that you download the Orweb browser during the Tor installation itself.

The advantage of using Orweb is that it requires absolutely no configuration by the user and once installed it is all set to connect to the Tor network. Once you have installed both Orbot and Orweb on your Android phone, you will notice that the following new icons will appear on your screen:

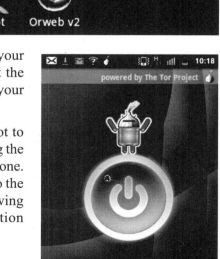

First of all you need to use Orbot to connect to the Tor network by starting the Orbot application on your Android phone. Once it has successfully connected to the Tor network, you will see the following message displayed on the application screen:

Now you are all set to start the Orweb browser and start browsing the Internet absolutely anonymously, safely and securely. You can even visit websites that may normally be blocked by your mobile operator, company or government.

If for some reason you don't like the Orweb browser and prefer to use the more familiar Firefox browser, then it is also possible for you to use Firefox for Android to connect to the Tor network. If you have a newer Android phone, then you can install Firefox for Android from the Android Marketplace and then install the ProxymobAddon (https://addons.mozilla.org/en-US/mobile/addon/251558/). Once installed, you will need to configure Firefox to connect to the tor network by connecting to the local proxy on 127.0.0.1, HTTP Port 8118 and SOCKS Port 9050. To configure these settings, you will need to go into Proxymob Add On Options > Proxy Settings.

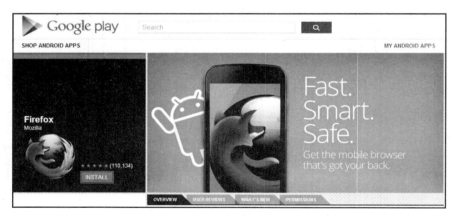

It is important to note that if you are using a rooted phone, then you don't need any specific browser application installed, since Orbot will send all data through the tor network automatically.

Irrespective of which browser you may choose to use, to check whether you have successfully managed to configure an anonymous connection to the tor network on your Android phone, you can simply connect tohttps://check.torproject. org/. If everything is working properly, then you will see the following message displayed on the screen. Otherwise, you may need to tweak the installation and make sure everything has been configured properly. I am going to use the Orweb browser in this example, since that is the simplest to use and requires the least amount of configuration.

Now that you have managed to connect tor to the tor network on your Android phone, all your Internet communication will be completely anonymous. Your company or government have no clue about which websites you are visiting on your mobile phone device and of course, if any websites are blocked, you will now be able to unblock them!

Let us now put Orbot and tor to test and see whether it is able to provide us with an absolutely anonymous connection on our Android phone or not. We can open a regular browser that is not configured to use Tor and try to connect to www.whatismyipaddress.com.

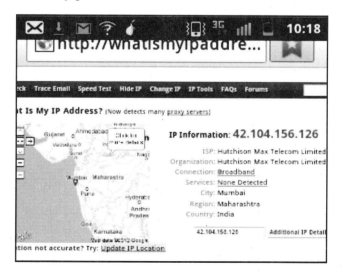

Within a few seconds, the website www.whatismyipaddress. com detects my IP address as 42.104.156.126 and my location as Mumbai, India. It has also detected that the mobile operator that I am currently using is Hutchison Max Telecom (also known as Vodafone). Clearly, my identity and location are known to every single website and web application that I use on my Android phone. Let me now try using the Orweb browser, which is configured to connect to tor and let us once again open the website www.whatismyipaddress.com. This time, the following appears on my Android screen:

If you notice, this time my IP address is completely hidden and my location has changed as well. Apparently, now my IP address is 31.172.30.4 and I am located in Al Khobar, Saudi Arabia. Now it is possible for you to visit all your favourite websites on the Internet absolutely anonymous, safely and securely. Not only that, if your company or government or mobile operator is blocking certain websites, then you can now go ahead and unblock them. Your company or government will think that you are merely connecting to a random tor server, but in reality you are using that to anonymously connect to blocked websites.

How to Unblock Instant Messengers and Anonymously Chat with your Friends using your Android Phone

In the previous section, we have seen how easy it is to configure your Android browser to connect to the tor network so that you can surf anonymously and access even blocked websites on the Internet. However, what if you are worried that your mobile phone operator, company or government is monitoring and maybe even blocking your Instant Messenger Chat activity on your mobile phone device? It is actually also possible to anonymously route your Instant Messenger traffic from your mobile phone through the Tor network.

There is a very useful application called Gibberbot that allows users to use Orbot's Tor on Android application to anonymously and securely connect to various Instant Messenger networks like Google, Facebook, any Jabber or XMPP server. It is possible to download and install the Gibberbot application from its official website (https://guardianproject.info/apps/gibber/) or from the Android Marketplace.

Once you have successfully installed the Gibberbot application, then simply start the Orbot application and make sure that you are connected to the Tor network.

Now you are ready to start the Gibberbot chat application to anonymously connect to the various popular chat networks. Not only will your identity details be now completely hidden and anonymous while you are chatting with your friends, but you will also be able to unblock access to any blocked chat networks.

26

How to Unblock Tor if it is Blocked

In the previous section, we have seen how easy it is to use Tor to become completely anonymous on the Internet and unblock access to blocked websites. However, in the last few years, with the rising popularity of the Tor application, a lot of colleges, companies and governments have started implementing strategies to block even Tor.

One of the most popular techniques to prevent the use of Tor is to block access to all the publicly known Tor relay servers. The complete list of tor relay servers can easily be accessed using the Vidalia Control Panel by clicking on the *View The Network* button. If a system administrator were to block all these tor servers, then Tor would stop working and you would not be able to connect to any blocked websites on the Internet. If tor relay servers have been blocked, then when you start the Tor software, you will get an error message saying something like *Could Not Connect to Tor Network*.

This is where something known as Bridge Relays come to the rescue! Bridge Relays are Tor Relay servers that are normally not published in the above mentioned public list of tor relay servers. In other words, bridge relay servers are secret or hidden servers that your college, company or government will not know about and would not have necessarily blocked. If tor relay servers have been blocked and you are unable to connect to tor, you need to find and start using Tor Bridge Relay Servers or Tor Bridges.

There are currently two different ways of finding Tor bridges:

1. If you visit the webpage https://bridges.torproject.org/ you will be able to get information about some new tor bridges, as shown below:

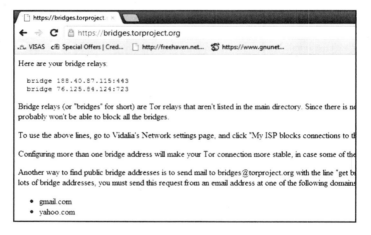

2. If for some reason, even the above webpage is blocked by your system administrator, you can even request for the tor bridges information to be sent to you by email. All you need to do is to send an email to bridges@bridges.torproject.org with the line *get bridges* in the body of the email. Make sure you send this email from a Gmail account, since any emails sent from other email accounts will not be accepted. Within a few minutes you should receive a reply containing some tor bridges that you can use.

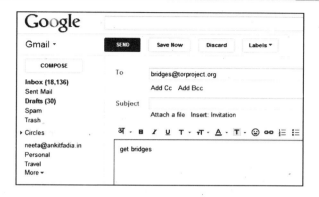

Once you have received the tor bridges information, you need to configure the Tor application to use these new bridges. Open the Vidalia Control Panel > Settings > Network and Select the option *My ISP Blocks connections to the Tor network*. In the box below, Tor will now allow you to add the IP addresses of the new Tor bridges by clicking on the PLUS button. It is recommended that you add as many new bridges to this list as possible to make it harder for your college, company or government to block you!

Since these new bridges that you are adding are not publicly published anywhere, chances are that they have not been blocked and you will be able to access all your favourite blocked websites on the Internet.

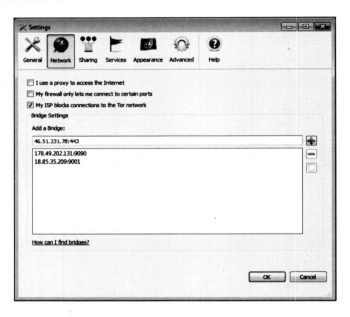

If your network administrator is blocking all the tor bridges as well (quite unlikely!), then it is also possible for you to run your own Tor Bridge on your home computer, add its information to the Vidalia Control of the Tor application in your office or college and then you will then be able to bypass any blocking that may have been implemented.

Some network administrators, in addition to blocking Tor relay servers will also block the various ports that Tor uses for communication. In such a case, it is also possible to force Tor to only use Port 80 and Port 443 for all its communication. Port 80 and Port 443 are normally not blocked by most colleges, companies and government. To configure this option, simply go to Vidalia Control Panel > Settings > Network and enable the option *My*

Firewall only lets me connect to certain Ports. On most occasions, this will resolve the problem and allow you to continue to use Tor by unblocking Tor!

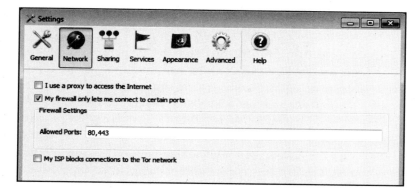

Freegate

Freegate is a software primarily design to help people in countries where governments censor the Internet quite tightly (like China, Iran, Myanmar, UAE, Saudi Arabia and others) to bypass the restrictions and access blocked websites. It has been developed by a group called Dynamic Internet Technology. They have a large number of proxy servers located in different parts of the world, using which they allow their users to unblock stuff on the Internet. It is completely free for users within China. However, for users outside China this is shareware software, which you need to buy after the trial period gets over. It can be downloaded from http://www.dit-inc.us/freegate.

Like most other anti-censorship software, Freegate is very easy to install. At the end of the installation process, Freegate will automatically open a new secure Internet Explorer window that can be used to access blocked websites absolutely anonymously, safely and securely.

Once you start Freegate, this is what the interface looks like (see next screenshot). It will automatically connect to its directory server and download the latest list of proxy servers that it can connect to and will establish a secure connection for you. Internet Explorer by default is preconfigured to be used securely to connect to blocked websites. However, if you want to use any other browsers or applications through Freegate, then you need to change their proxy settings such that they connect to Freegate on Port 8580 on the location system 127.0.0.1.

Once Freegate starts, it makes sense to test the connection out and make sure it works by connecting to the website http://www.whatismyipaddress.com. It immediately tells you that the IP address that has been given to you is 65.49.2.185 and look at the location in the screenshot below! Like in the case of Ultrasurf, it is once again off the coast of Africa in the middle of the ocean. Now your connection is secure, safe and you can start accessing blocked content on the Internet.

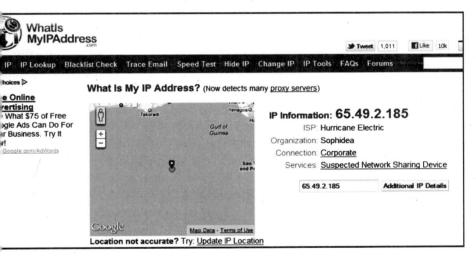

Freegate is very popular in China, as it is one of the most effective methods of bypassing the Chinese government's blocking firewall. And trust me, if it works in China, it will probably work in most companies, colleges and organizations in other parts of the world.

DynaWeb

If everything else fails, then you can usually always rely on DynaWeb to come to your rescue and allow you to access blocked websites. DynaWeb comes from the same team that brought you Freegate. It is one of the largest collection of web proxies in the world that allows users to bypass firewalls, censorship and other restrictions and access their favourite blocked websites on the Internet. DynaWeb has specifically been designed keeping in mind Chinese users who are constantly being censored by the Chinese government. As a result, it is extremely effective and reliable.

The Chinese government is constantly trying to block DynaWeb and all its various proxy servers. This forces DynaWeb to be very dynamic and fast in coming up with new IP addresses, domain names and other mechanisms to bypass the Chinese government restrictions and continue to provide uncensored Internet to users. According to their website, at any given point of time they have hundreds of mirrors of their web proxies running. As soon as they notice that one of their web proxies has been found out and blocked by the Chinese, they will immediately change its IP and domain name. It is a constant cat and mouse game between DynaWeb and the Chinese government, a game that DynaWeb is current winning by a big margin.

Just the way the Chinese government blocks websites, even your company, college, organization and government may also be blocking websites. Moreover, just the way the Chinese government blocks new techniques, proxies and domains, similarly even your company, college, organization and government are trying to figure out the new unblocking techniques you are using and then blocking them! But the good news is that if DynaWeb is able to fool the

Chinese government (which employs 1000s of people just to figure out which websites, domains and IP Addresses to block), they will probably be able to fool even your company, college, organization and government quite easily. Please note that on many occasions while testing DynaWeb, I have noticed that after a certain period of time of free usage, it will not allow users from outside China to continue using their services. So just keep that in mind.

There are multiple ways to access the proxy servers of DynaWeb:

- Domain Names
- Email
- FreeGate Client

DynaWeb has created a bunch of domain names (usually with quite unusual names that organizations normally would not think about blocking) that you can type into your browser to access their web proxies, which can then be used to connect to blocked websites on the Internet. The most current domain names that are using are listed below. The beauty of the DynaWeb system is that they keep changing the domain names they use for their proxies, which means that by the time you read this, the below domain may or may not be valid. You can always visit their website to get details about the most current web proxies that they are using.

http://wd.carnivore.pl/

http://fc.multicop.com.ar/

http://tq.12c.pp.ru/

http://us.dongtaiwang.com/home_en.php

If you open any of the above listed web proxies in your browser, you are likely to be greeted by a webpage in the Chinese language like the following:

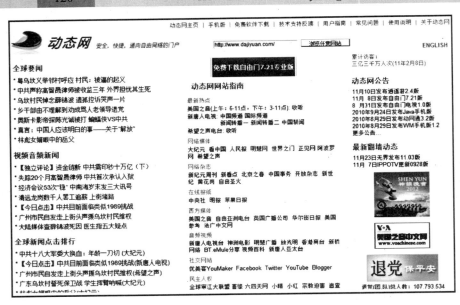

If you are like me, you probably cannot read even a bit of the Mandarin Chinese language. Once you have connected to this website, then in the input box you should type the blocked website address that you want to visit anonymously and then click on whatever looks like the GO button. Within a few seconds, the website that you have requested should show up on the screen. No need to know how to read the Chinese language. Or you could simply click on the ENGLISH link on the right hand top corner, which should take you to the English version of the same website:

This English version of the DynaWeb website is probably a lot easier to understand. In the space provided, simply type the blocked website you want to unblock and click on the Anonymous Surfing button. I have just typed in http://www.whatismyipaddress.com and within a few seconds we get the following result:

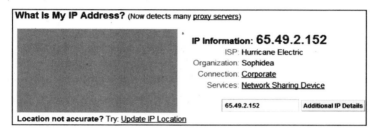

On many occasions, it may not be possible to visit DynaWeb to get access to the latest domain names of their web proxy servers since your government, company or college may have blocked it. This is where their email service comes so handy. If a user sends a blank email to DynaWeb at d_ip@dongtaiwang. com, then within a few minutes they will send back a reply, containing the IP addresses of the some of the their latest most current web proxy servers:

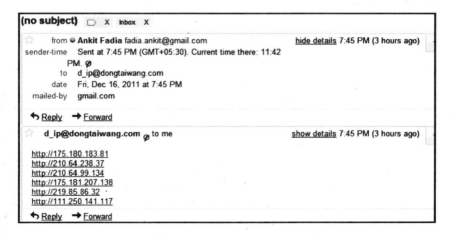

It is possible for a user to connect to any of these web proxies to bypass the local firewall restriction and connect to blocked websites on the Internet. Just click on any of the links you received via email or type them in your browser and you will be taken to the DynaWeb website which will then allow you to access blocked content on the Internet. Now you need to follow exactly the same procedure that was followed while connecting to the domain name web proxies of DynaWeb.

The last and one of the best methods of connecting to any of the DynaWeb proxies is using their client software called Freegate. We have already discussed FreeGate in detail in the previous section.

29   Hide My IP

This is yet another tool which, once installed on your computer, will allow you to bypass censorship, hide your identity and surf the Internet anonymously. All applications on your computer can be configured to filter through the local firewall by connecting to Hide My IP. It is available as a 14-day trial download from http://www.hide-my-ip.com/ after which you have to pay for it and buy it.

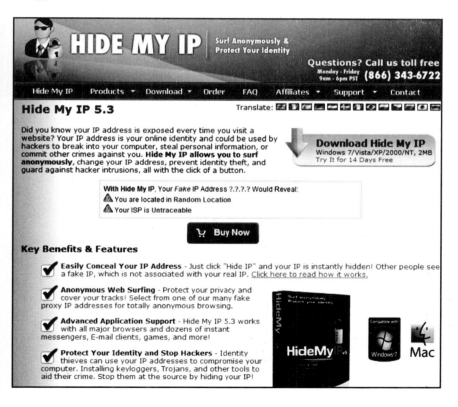

⬡ 30   JonĐo IP Changer

JonDo IP changer is a tool that you can install on your computer and it will allow you to change your identity, surf anonymously and even access blocked websites on the Internet. JonDo is absolutely free and has been written in JAVA. Once installed on your computer, it will open Port 4001 on your computer and you need to configure all web applications on your computer to connect to the JonDo proxy on Port 4001 of your own computer to access blocked stuff on the Internet. Let us now quickly see the steps that you need to follow to use JonDo IP Changer to unblock websites and be anonymous on the Internet:

STEP 1: Download JonDo IP changer from http://anonymous-proxy-servers.net/en/jondo.html and install on it on your computer

STEP 2: Once JonDo is successfully installed on your computer, it will prompt you to configure all your web applications to connect to Port 4001 on the local system. We have already seen in the previous examples how easy it is to do that.

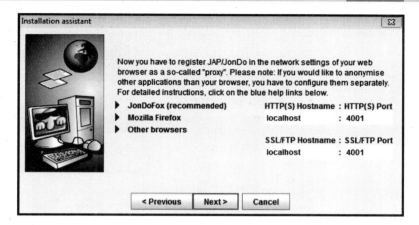

STEP 3: Within a few seconds after installation and configuration, the JonDo application will connect to a random proxy server from its database of known proxies and will establish an anonymous connection for you:

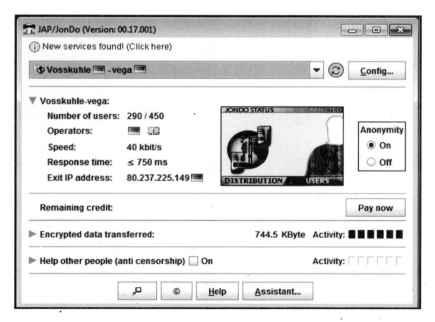

STEP 4: Once the connection has been established we can do a quick check to see if our connection is truly anonymous and secure by opening the website http://www. whatismyipddress.com:

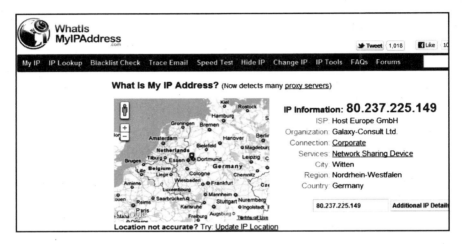

Now you can enjoy unblocked, unrestricted and anonymous Internet access to all your favourite websites and applications. The only problem with JonDo is that when I tested it on a few machines it drastically slowed down the computer and gave relatively slow Internet access through its proxies. However, if all you need to unblock basic websites on the Internet which do not require too much bandwidth, then this is perfect.

<table>
<tr><td>

31

</td><td>

Green Simurgh

</td></tr>
</table>

It is a simple, fast and easy-to-use proxy software that can be downloaded free of cost from the Internet. It does not need to be installed on your computer and is in fact a standalone EXE file, which can be directly run from a USB pen drive, camera, music player and does not even require any configuration to be done. It will automatically configure your browser to connect through its proxy server and give you secure anonymous access to blocked websites on the Internet. As simple as that! Simurgh means *phoenix* in the Persian language and was originally created with the objective to provide unblocked Internet access to people in Iran. However, nowadays users across the world are using it to unblock stuff on the Internet. The various steps involved in using Green Simurgh are the following:

STEP 1: Green Simurgh is a free proxy software that can be downloaded from the website https://simurghesabz.net (the entire website is in Persian but still quite easy to use for everybody from different parts of the world). The best part about the Green Simurgh is that it does not require any installation or any configuration. It can be run directly from a standalone EXE file, hence leaving no traces behind on the system.

STEP 2: Double click on the downloaded EXE file and automatically the Green Simurgh software will start. It will automatically make the necessary changes in the browser settings and will open a brand new window in Internet Explorer which will show you your new IP Address.

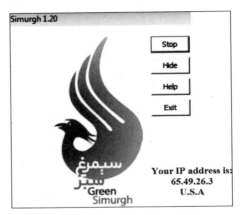

Opening a browser window to http://www. whatismyipaddress.com confirms that your identity and location have been changed and you can now access blocked websites on the Internet through the Green Simurgh proxy server.

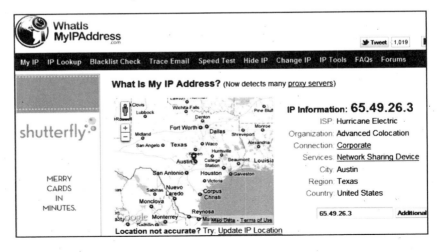

By default the Green Simurgh proxy works with only Internet Explorer. However, it is also possible to use all other web applications with Simurgh by configuring them to connect to it on Port 2048 on the local system. For example, on Google Chrome, simply click on TOOLS wrench icon > Options > Under the Hood > Change Proxy Settings button > Settings Button > Enable the USE PROXY SERVER option and enter the IP address 127.0.0.1 and Port Number 2048. As simple as that!

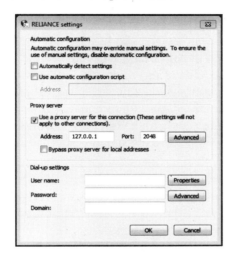

32 Alkasir

Alkasir is yet another censorship circumvention or unblocking software that can be installed on your computer. It has proxy servers in different parts of the world that it uses to provide users access to blocked content on the Internet. It is available as a free download on the Internet from its website http://www.alkasir.com. It was originally created to help users, especially in the Middle East, to bypass government filters and access blocked website. But in reality it can be used by anybody in any part of the world. Once installed on your computer, it allows you to unblock websites and have an anonymous secure access to the Internet. It works quite similar to some of the other software discussed earlier in this book.

| | Home | About | Downloads | Censorship Map | Conta |

alkasir for Mapping and Circumventing Cyber-Censorship

Languages
- العربية
- English

ankitfadia
- My account
- Send invitations to others
- Log out

Build 1.2.462 released

Mon, 09/05/2011 - 22:34 — alkasir

We've just released build 462 of version 1.2 for alkasir circumvention software. Th
after a standby or hibernation. In earlier versions, we were told there were proble
Hopefully, this build solves this issue.

If you have questions or concerns, please don't hesitate to contact us.

alkasir team

33 ⬡　　　　　　　　　　　　Easy Hide IP

Most websites nowadays are tracking the activities of visitors. If you want to protect your identity and make sure that websites are not able track your identity, then a very good solution is an application known as Easy Hide IP. It can obviously also be used to unblock access to any websites that your college or company may have blocked. If you use Easy Hide IP, then all your traffic gets routed via an encrypted connection through their remote servers. Your network will think that you are simply connecting to a random remote server, but in reality you will be using that remote server to access all your favourite blocked websites on the Internet. It is possible to download a 3-day trial version of the Easy Hide IP software (and of course to buy it as well) from http://www.easy-hide-ip.com/.

After an easy installation process, Easy Hide IP is ready to be used. The interface of this application is extremely user friendly and easy to use. At the top left corner of the screen, it will display your computer's current IP address. In this case, my computer's current IP address is 59.161.42.179. My personal favourite feature in the Easy Hide IP application is the fact that it allows you to choose the country through which you wish to connect to the Internet. In other words, using this software it is possible for you to pretend to be in any part of the world, be it Australia, Canada, Germany, Denmark, Spain or others!

In this example, I would like to change my IP address and pretend to be in Canada. I am going to click on the CONNECT button next to the relevant country listing. Within a few seconds, EASY HIDE IP creates an encrypted communication channel through that particular selected server and automatically configures your browser to route all traffic via their server. Now if I open my browser and connect to the website http://whatismyipaddress.com/ if you notice my IP address and location have changed to: 74.82.193.152 in Hamilton, Ontario, Canada.

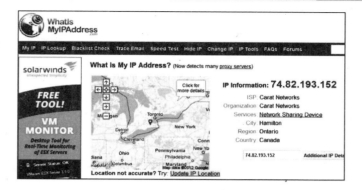

The Easy Hide IP application also allows users to automatically change their IP address on a periodic interval basis, hence, making it almost impossible for your identity to be tracked. As soon as you run Easy Hide IP, it will automatically configure your browser to send all traffic through the Easy Hide IP server. However, if you are using some application other than your browser and want even its traffic to be routed via the Easy Hide IP application, then simply click on Program Settings and add the application to the list!

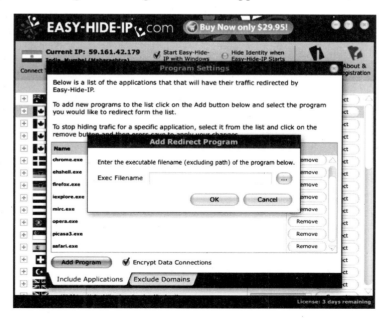

It is also possible to configure Easy Hide IP in such a way that traffic to certain domain names will go directly instead of being routed via the Easy Hide IP servers. This may be desired if you wish to reveal your real identity to certain trusted domain names. To enable this option, all you need to do is click on Program Settings > Exclude Domains option and then add all the trusted domains to the list:

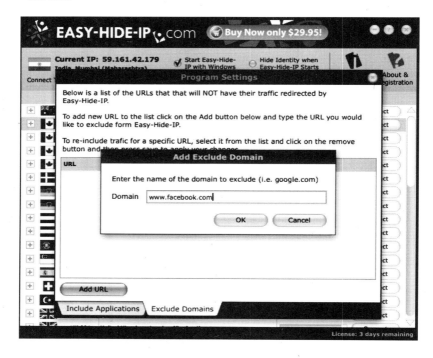

34 Mask Surf Pro

Mask Surf Pro is a very easy-to-use application that allows users to setup anonymous and secure tunnels on the Internet through which private communication can be carried out. It can obviously also be used to unblock access to those websites that may have been blocked by a system administrator. In the backend, Mask Surf Pro makes uses of the immensely popular anonymizing tool tor that we have discussed earlier in this book. Mask Surf Pro is easy to setup, automatically configures browsers, allows users to choose which country to bounce off from and has many inbuilt anonymity tests as well. It is possible to download Mask Surf Pro from http://www.thanksoft.com/

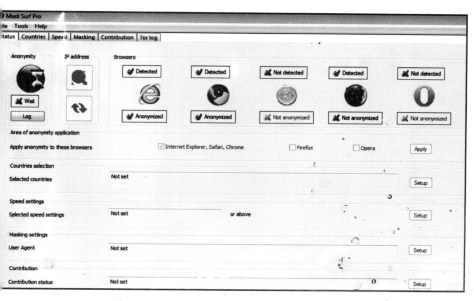

Quick Hide IP Platinum

Quick Hide IP Platinum is a proxy application that allows users to connect to its proxy servers in the US and Europe to hide their IP address. The 3-day trial edition of this application can be downloaded from http://www.quick-hide-ip.com/ and it is extremely easy to install and setup. The best part about the application is that it does not require users to do any configuration in the browsers. Quick Hide IP Platinum is ready to use as soon as it is installed. Once you run the Quick Hide IP Platinum application, this is what will get displayed on the screen. At the right bottom corner of the screen, it will display your current IP address.

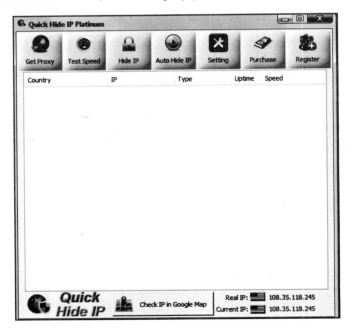

Now click on the GET PROXY button to download a complete list of proxy servers available to Quick Hide IP Platinum.

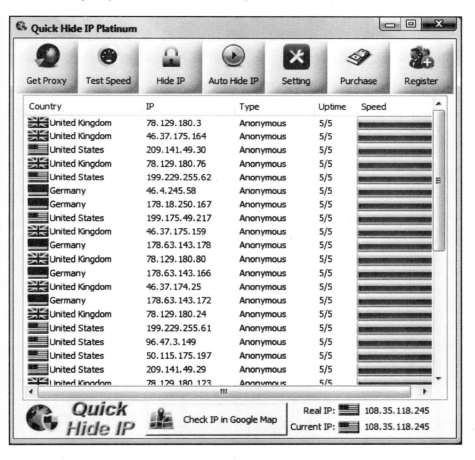

Select any proxy server of your choice from the list and then click on the HIDE IP button and Quick Hide IP Platinum will automatically connect to it. If you look at the right bottom corner, you will notice that your IP address has now been changed. Not only does Quick Hide IP Platinum hide your IP address, it also allows you unblock access to blocked websites on the Internet. As simple as that!

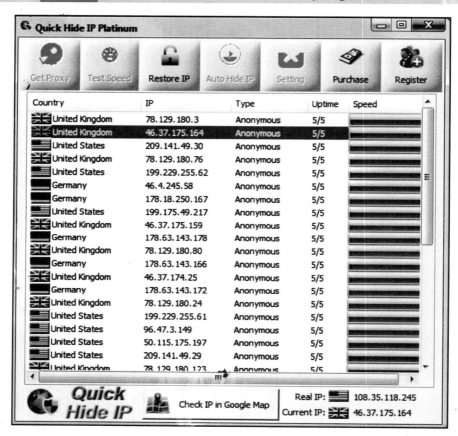

Browser Add-Ons and Extensions

Popular browsers like Mozilla Firefox and Google Chrome have something known as browser add- ons or extensions. (Mozilla Firefox likes to call them add-ons and Google Chrome likes to call them extensions, but they are both essentially the same thing). Browser add-ons or extensions are scripts or utilities that run within your browser and add new features or functionality to your browsing experience. They usually give you more control over your browsing experience. Most of the extensions or add-ons are free and can be installed within a few seconds within your browser. You can search, browse and download them from:

- Mozilla Firefox Add-Ons - https://addons.mozilla.org
- Google Chrome Extensions – http://chrome.google.com/extensions

There are numerous browser add-ons and extensions that are available which allow you to connect to the Internet through a proxy server, anonymize your connection and unblock blocked websites, all with a single click of the mouse button. No need to download any proxy tool or to configure your browser to connect to a proxy server. All you need to do instead is install a browser add-on or extension within your browser and start browsing anonymously with a single click of the mouse button.

STEP 1: Open your browser (I am going to use Mozilla Firefox for this example, but the exact same process can be followed in Google Chrome and other popular browsers as well) and connect to the Mozilla Firefox add ons website at https://addons.mozilla.org. Using this website you can search, browse and install any add-on of your choice in your browser. Let us search for the keyword proxy and see what comes up:

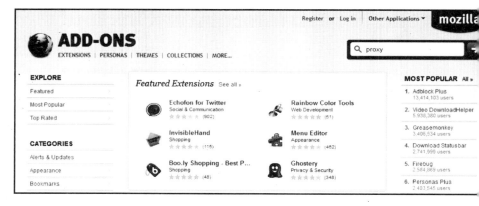

STEP 2: Within a few seconds, it will show up a bunch of add on scripts that you can install in your browser using which you can connect to proxy servers on the Internet. Scroll down and select any add-on script of your choice. I am going to go ahead and download and install the add-on called *Hide My Ass! Web Proxy.* Some other popular proxy related add-on tools available on Mozilla Firefox are FoxyProxy Standard, Quick Proxy, Proxy Tool and others.

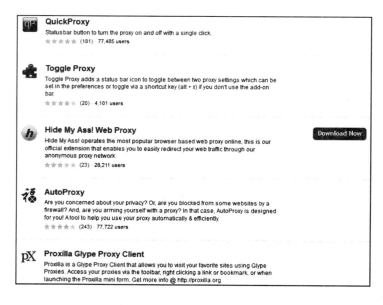

STEP 3: Once you have installed the *Hide My Ass Web Proxy* add-on in your Mozilla Firefox browser, you will notice that in the URL address bar a new *Hide My Ass* button (with the letter H) has been added.

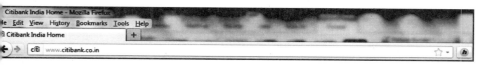

Whenever you want to access a website normally without a proxy server, then you simply type the website address in the URL address bar and press enter as you normally would. However, in case you want to connect to a website through a proxy server, you need to click on the *Hide My Ass* button and then type the website URL address in the space that gets displayed on the screen. Your IP address will automatically change and you will be connected to the website of your choice via the *Hide My Ass* proxy server. In case a particular website is blocked, then you will be able to access it as well. In the screenshots below, I am going to connect to www.whatismyipaddress.com two times. The first time I will connect to it directly and the second time I will connect to it after pressing the *Hide My Ass* button.

CASE 1: Connecting to www.whatismyipaddress.com directly from the browser reveals your real IP address and location.

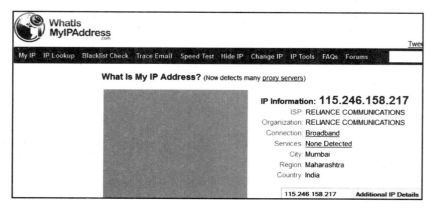

CASE 2: Connecting to www.whatismyipaddress.com by pressing the *Hide My Ass* button reveals a fake IP address of a proxy server in the United States.

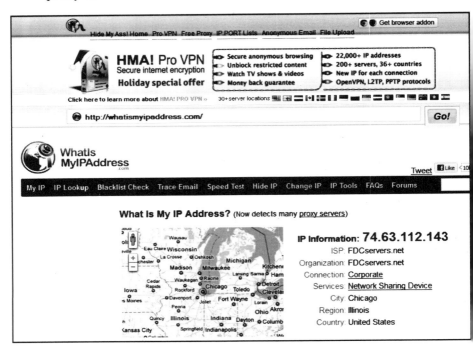

Cocoon

Cocoon is an app that runs in the form of a Browser Add On and a web application that allows users to browse the Internet absolutely anonymously and privately. It is available as a free download from https://getcocoon.com and currently available for Internet Explorer, Firefox and iPhone/iPad platforms. After installation, Cocoon requires users to create an account, which is quite a straightforward and simple process.

Once installed, Cocoon provides the following security and privacy features to users:

- Protects against tracking websites
- Keeps history private
- Provides encrypted browsing

- Hides IP address
- Unblocks blocked websites
- Provides antivirus and malware protection

On my computer, I have installed Cocoon on the Firefox browser, but the Google Chrome browser does not have Cocoon installed. When I open the Google Chrome browser and connect to the website www.whatismyipaddress.com, the IP address that shows up is 108.35.118.245 and the location is Jersey City, New Jersey, USA.

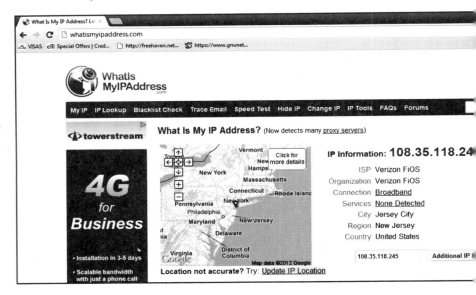

Now, if I open the Firefox browser (that has the Cocoon plugin installed) and connect to the www.whatismyipaddress.com website, then if you notice my IP address and location has changed to 64.71.142.140 in Milipitas, California, USA.

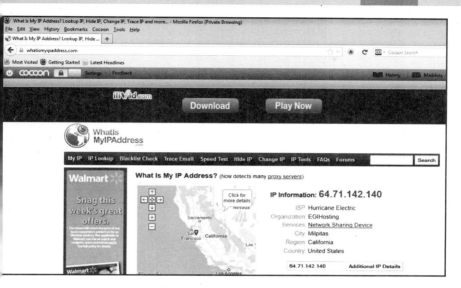

Not only does Cocoon make your Internet connection anonymous, but it also allows you access websites which normally may be blocked by your college, company or government.

⬡ 38 ⬡   Secure VPNs

A VPN stands for a Virtual Private Network and is typically used by companies and organizations to allow their employees to remotely connect to their central office network from anywhere on the Internet. For example, let us assume that you work for a company that is headquartered in Singapore. If you are travelling in Japan or United States or Brazil for work and want to access files, folders, database, printers and other network resources back in your Singapore headquarters, then you can use VPN.

Such VPNs can also be used to bypass any blocking or censorship of websites that may have been done by your college or company's network. Instead of accessing the Internet through the censored and filtered firewall of your network, it is possible to get unrestricted full access to the Internet by simply establishing a HTTPS encrypted VPN connection to a public VPN service!

One of my favourite Secure VPN service is HotSpot Shield (http://hotspotshield.com). HotSpot Shield is a free VPN service (supported by some basic light ads) that establishes an HTTPS encrypted VPN connection between your computer and their Internet gateway, hence giving you full unrestricted to access to everything on the Internet. Your local network thinks that you are connecting to a random harmless server on the Internet. In reality, you are using that secure encrypted connection to access blocked content on the Internet.

Hotspot Shield can be downloaded from http://hotspotshield.com and installation does not take more than a few minutes. Once Hotspot Shield has been installed on your computer, you can launch it to tunnel all Internet traffic from your computer through their secure HTTPS VPN service. No configuration or changing of settings is required.

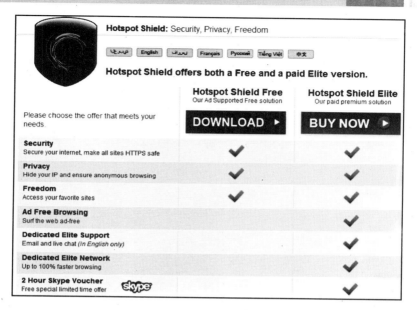

Now when you launch any application on your computer, it will automatically route your Internet access through the VPN service of Hotspot Shield. A quick connection to http://www.whatismyipaddress.com reveals my IP address as 64.145.82.169 and my location as California, USA even though I am actually in India!

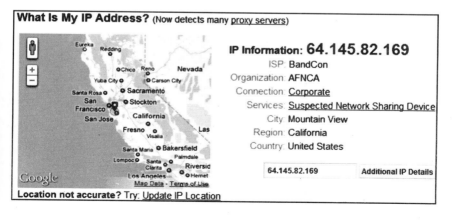

Once you are done with your work, you can disconnect from the HotSpot Shield VPN network by clicking on its icon in the taskbar notification area.

39   Premium VPN Services

We have already seen how to get encrypted anonymous Internet access using a VPN. There are plenty of free VPN services available on the Internet. Unfortunately, some of the free VPN services sometimes put a restriction on the speed of your connection, level of encryption and may even display some ads. In this section, we will discuss some premium VPN services that provide some advance features and more control over your encrypted anonymous Internet connection.

One of my favourite premium VPN services on the Internet is an application called Hide My Ass Pro VPN (https://www.hidemyass.com) or HMA Pro VPN. This is not a free service. It comes with a monthly price tag of around $10 (approximately ₹ 500), but there are a lot of advance features built into the software.

Like any other VPN software, the primary objective of the HMA Pro VPN is to provide users with a secure encrypted anonymous access to the Internet. It is extremely easy to install. Once installed, with a single click of the mouse button, automatically all your Internet access and communication become secure. There is no need to manually configure any of your web applications individually. According to their website, HMA PRO VPN has more than 22,500 different IP Addresses located in 36 different countries that you can choose from. Imagine the kind of flexibility it gives you in terms of being able to choose which country you want to seem to be located in. Each time you connect to HMA Pro VPN, you will be given a new IP address and the best part is, if you don't like your current allocated IP address for some reason then you can change it very easily. There are no ads, no bandwidth restrictions, no spyware and no unnecessary nonsense. The best part about this software is that it is really fast and of course you can use it to unblock stuff on the Internet.

Once you have created an account on the HMA Pro VPN website, it will email you a link, from which you can download the software. Installation is a breeze and there is no configuration you need to do on any of your applications. Once you launch the application, you will be greeted by the dashboard which allows you to change all the settings related to your VPN connection. Enter your username and password and click on the Connect to VPN button to start your secure encrypted anonymous connection.

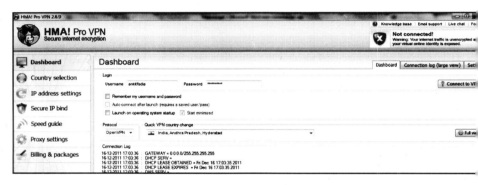

Once you have connected to the VPN, the first thing you should do is to check if your connection is truly secure and anonymous or not. This can be done easily by clicking on the IP Address Settings button in the left navigation bar > Select a website you wish to use to check your IP address > Click on the Verify IP address button. Within a few seconds the selected website will show up on your computer screen showing you your current IP address and location, which in this case happens to be 175.101.0.70 and Hyderabad, India. (My real IP address is something else and my real location is Mumbai, India.)

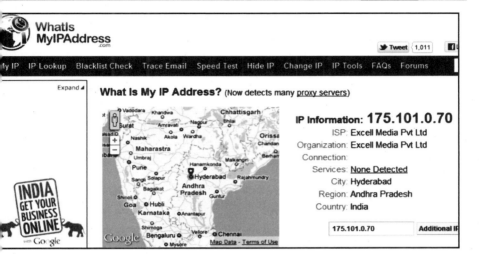

HMA VPN Pro makes it very easy for users to change their IP address to any other IP of their choice by just selecting one from a drop down list. In the below screenshot we use the Dashboard to change our IP address to an address in Singapore.

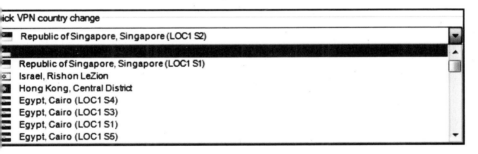

There is also an option under IP Address Settings that allows users to automatically change their IP address at predefined periodic intervals without any manual intervention.

Overall, HMA Pro VPN is very reliable, has some pretty cool features, is quite fast and does a great job of protecting your identity and allowing you to bypass the filtering mechanism of your college, company or organization.

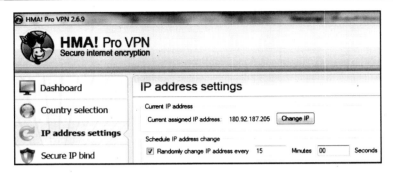

Some other premium VPN services that are available on the Internet are the following:

- Express VPN (https://www.express-vpn.com)
- Strong VPN (http://www.strongvpn.com)
- Vyper VPN (http://www.vyprvpn.com)
- Security Kiss (http://www.securitykiss.com)
- OpenVPN (http://openvpn.net)

40   Popular VPN Services

In the previous section, we have seen how easy it is for users to use a VPN service to circumvent any censorship or blocking that may have been implemented by a college, company or government. Below are some more popular VPN services that are highly recommended:

VPN Service	Website
12vpn	https://12vpn.com/
GoTrusted	http://www.gotrusted.com/
WiTopia	https://www.witopia.net/
Switch VPN	https://switchvpn.net/
Strong VPN	http://strongvpn.com/
ibVPN	http://www.ibvpn.com/
Astrill	https://www.astrill.com/
IP Shield	http://ip-shield.net/
Cyber Ghost VPN	http://cyberghostvpn.com/
Box VPN	http://www.boxpn.com
VyprVPN	http://www.goldenfrog.com/vyprvpn
Your Freedom	https://www.your-freedom.net/
Security Kiss	http://www.securitykiss.com/
IP Vanish	http://www.ipvanish.com
Open VPN	http://openvpn.net/
Tsunagarumon	http://www.tsunagarumon.com
USA IP	http://www.usaip.eu
Expat Shield	http://www.expatshield.com/
Pro XPN	https://proxpn.com/
Garden Networks	http://gardennetworks.org/
Gapp Proxy	http://code.google.com/p/gappproxy/
HYK Proxy	http://code.google.com/p/hyk-proxy/
GPass	http://gpass1.com/gpass/

41   Psiphon

Psiphon is a fantastic service that allows users to access everything on the Internet by bypassing firewalls, filtering devices, restrictions and blocking mechanisms. Psiphon is an advanced form of a web proxy which also utilizes some of the best practices that are seen in Tor and Ultrasurf. Psiphon allows users to unblock content on the Internet without the need to install anything or configure anything on their computers. Psiphon has a web interface where you can enter the address of the website you wish to visit anonymously or unblock. This HTTP request for a webpage is encrypted and obfuscated and sent to the Psiphon proxy server, which will in turn rewrite the request and send it to the actual destination and then send back the reply to the user. The replies are rewritten in such a way that all subsequent requests sent by the user will automatically pass through the Psiphon anonymous and unblocking system.

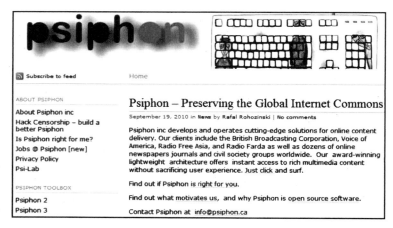

Originally, Psiphon was an invitation-only service that you could get invited to only if you knew somebody who was already using it. Now Psiphon has slowly opened itself up to everybody who wants to access blocked content on the Internet. The web interface of Psiphon can be accessed by simply opening your browser and connecting to the website http://psiphon.ca and clicking on the relevant link. In case your administrator has blocked access to this website as well, then it is possible to connect to an obfuscated URL and access Psiphon through it. The most current obfuscated URL that can be used to access the Psiphon website is: https://687110.info/001/. The best part about Psiphon is that they keep changing their web interface URL or web address very regularly so that users can continue to access it even if Psiphon gets blocked by the users' companies, colleges or governments. It is highly recommended that you create an account on Psiphon so that they can keep informing you via email about their latest obfuscated interface addresses as well. So never ever get blocked again, no matter which college, company or organization you are a part of. Once you connect to the web interface of Psiphon you will be greeted with the following welcome message:

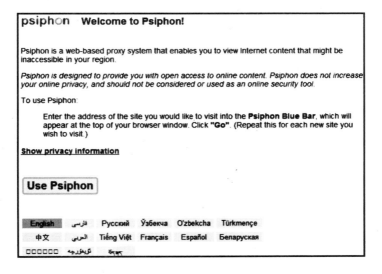

When you click on the USE PSIPHON button, a new browser window will open with the *Psiphon Blue* bar at the top where you can type any website address that you wish to unblock and access anonymously. For example in the screenshot below I have just used the Psiphon Blue bar to access Facebook even though it is blocked by my system administrator. In future all websites that you wish to unblock you should type in the Psiphon Blue bar instead of typing them in the browser address bar:

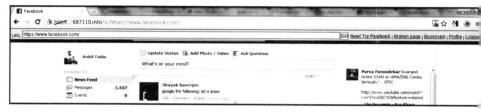

If you were to use the Psiphon Blue bar to connect to the website http://www.whatismyipaddress.com, you will notice that your IP address has changed to 69.10.234.58 and my location has changed to Oregan, United States:

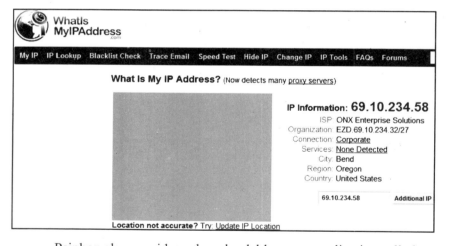

Psiphon also provides a downloadable proxy application called PsiphonX that routes all your web activity automatically through the Psiphon proxy. As soon as you run PsiphonX, it will automatically change your browser settings to make it connect to the Psiphon proxy server. You can control PsiphonX with a simple interface that it starts in your browser automatically:

Anonymous Peer-to-Peer Communication Networks

In this book, we have discussed a variety of techniques that enable users to unblock websites and circumvent censorship implemented by governments, companies and colleges. However, the fact remains that even such unblocking mechanisms (proxies, tor, Ultrasurf and others) can still be blocked, removed or attacked. This has led to the development of a few anonymous peer-to-peer communication networks that allow users to communicate and exchange files with each other completely anonymously and securely. Think of them as the anonymous and secure version of popular peer-to-peer file sharing networks like BitTorrent.

One of the oldest and most popular anonymous peer-to-peer communication networks is Freenet (https://freenetproject.org). Think of Freenet as a peer-to-peer network that allows users to store, exchange and distribute files with other Freenet users in a secure and anonymous fashion. Storage space is volunteered and provided by the various Freenet users themselves as a percentage of their hard disk space.

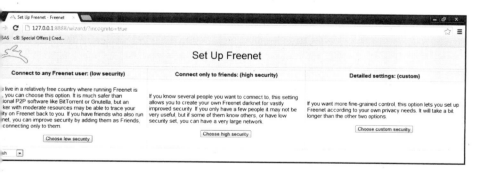

All files are stored on various users' or peers' computers in a secure encrypted manner. Each file stored by a user on the Freeet network has a key associated with it. This key can then be shared with other users who wish to retrieve and download the respective file. Since the identity of both the publisher and viewer of files is protected in Freenet, a lot of people use Freenet to share files anonymously and securely. Especially those files that are likely to be blocked or censored by the government.

I2P or the Invisible Internet Project is yet another anonymous communication network that allows users to communicate with each other anonymously and securely without revealing the identity of any of the users. It is an open source software and is available as a free download from http://www.i2p2.de. I2P is designed in such a way that it allows other applications (like browsing, email, file transfers and others) to communicate anonymously using the I2P software.

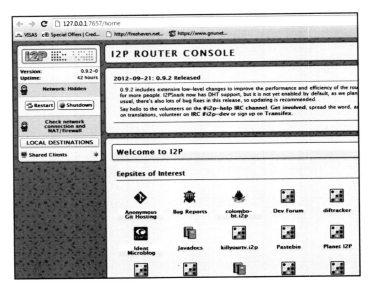

How to Unblock Websites on your iPad or iPhone

I am a big fan of Apple products and love using my iPad for all my entertainment and work purposes whenever I am on the move. However, I also travel to certain parts of the world (like China, Middle East and Africa), where, unfortunately, the respective local governments like to block and censor a lot of websites. Or sometimes when I connect to WiFi networks in colleges and companies using my iPad, unfortunately I face the censorship and firewall blocks that prevent me from accessing all the fun websites like Facebook, YouTube, Twitter and others. Desperate times like these call for desperate measures. It is time to see how easy it is to unblock access to blocked websites on the iPad using a Proxy Server or a VPN network.

STEP 1: On the home screen of your iPad or iPhone, let us first start the Safari Browser and open the website www.whatismyipaddress.com to check my current IP address. Presently, my IP address is showing as 108.35.118.245 and my location is showing as Jersey City, New Jersey, USA. Let us assume that my company, college or government has blocked access to certain websites. If you want to continue to access those blocked websites, then I need to configure my iPad to connect to a proxy server or VPN network.

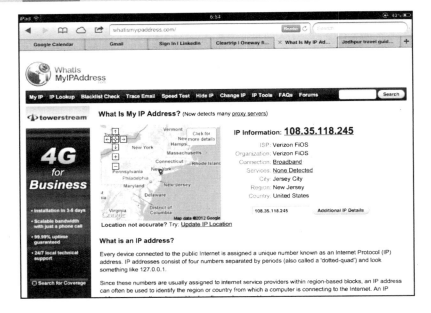

STEP 2: On the home screen of your iPad, select the Settings button.

STEP 3: Press the Wi-Fi option on the left panel and then select the right arrow button next to the Wi-Fi network that you are presently connected to. This will reveal the more advanced configuration options for the Wi-Fi network.

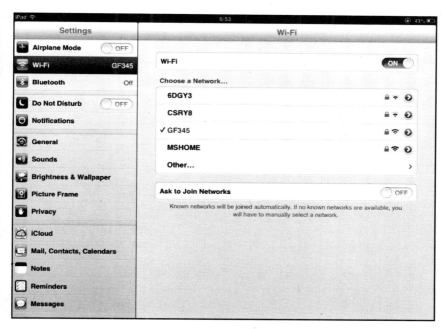

STEP 4: At the bottom, under the HTTP Proxy section, enable the MANUAL option and then enter the IP address and Port Number of the proxy server that you want your iPad to connect to. You can get Proxy Server details from any of the numerous Proxy Server Lists that we discussed earlier in this book (for example, www.hidemyass.com). In this case, I am going to enter 190.221.1.184 as the proxy server address and 3128 as the Port Number. Now my iPad is configured to connect to a proxy server.

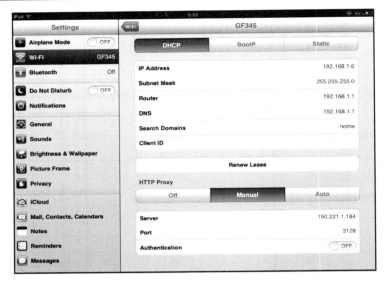

STEP 5: Let us now once again open the website www. whatismyipaddress.com in the Safari browser and let us see what output it shows.

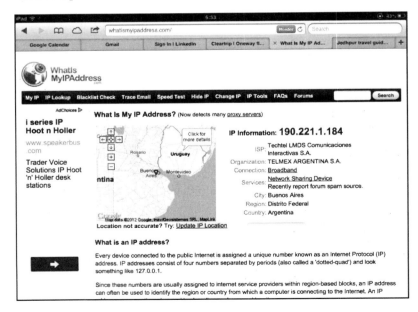

You will notice that the IP address and location have now changed to 190.221.1.184 in Buenos Aires, Argentina! It is now possible to use the iPad to connect to websites that are normally blocked by your company, college or government.

Instead of a proxy server, it is also possible to configure an iPad to connect to a VPN service to unblock access to blocked websites on the Internet. Simply select Settings > General > VPN > Add VPN Configuration and enter the VPN details.

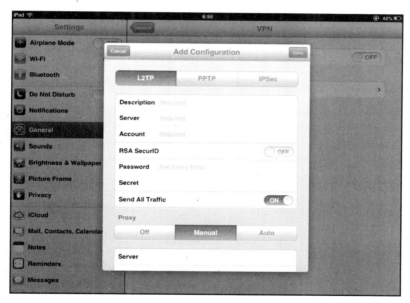

How to Watch American TV Shows Streaming for Free

Hulu.com is a video streaming website that allows users to legally watch American TV shows in HD quality online for free just a few days after they are broadcasted on television. Yes, it is completely legal. Yes, it is completely free. The only problem is that you have to be located in the United States to be able to do this legally and without paying any money for it. It is not currently available for users outside the United States. What do you do if you are not in the US and still want to watch American TV shows in HD quality for free on Hulu.com?

This is where everything that you have learnt in this book comes handy. Using any of the numerous techniques discussed in this book, you need to somehow pretend to be located in the United States. If you are able to do that, you will also be able to watch all your favourite American TV shows in HD quality on Hulu.com without paying any money.

In this example, I am going to use Hotspot Shield to VPN to a server based in the United States. A quick check on http://www.whatismyipaddress.com tells me that my IP address has changed to 64.145.82.169 and my location has changed to Mountain View, California, United States.

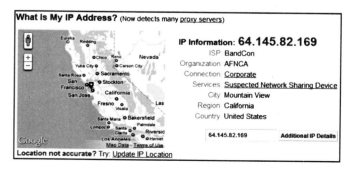

Now that I have successfully changed my location to a United States server, I can connect to http://www.hulu.com and watch all my favourite American TV shows for free. I love the TV show *Family Guy* and I am able to watch one of the latest episodes for free in HD quality for free by pretending to be in the United States. It is also possible to connect your laptop to your LCD or Plasma TV to watch the HD quality episodes on the big screen with surround sound audio.

⬡ 45   How to Unblock Pandora

Pandora (http://www.pandora.com) is a popular recommendation Internet radio service that plays songs similar to an initial song that a user selects. For every song that Pandora plays, users can provide negative or positive feedback which is taking into account while selecting future recommended songs. According to their website, Pandora analyses hundreds of attributes associated with a song (like melody, harmony, instrumentation, rhythm, vocals, lyrics and others) to come up with similar recommended songs. Although Pandora is completely free, it is unfortunately only available to users located within the United States. This can be quite frustrating. If anybody from outside the United States tries to access the Pandora website then they are greeted with an error message:

PANDORA

Dear Pandora Visitor,

We are deeply, deeply sorry to say that due to licensing constraints, we can no longer allow access to Pandora for listeners located outside of the U.S. We will continue to work diligently to realize the vision of a truly global Pandora, but for the time being we are required to restrict its use. We are very sad to have to do this, but there is no other alternative.

We believe that you are in **India** (your IP address appears to be **115.246.141.102**). If you believe we have made a mistake, we apologize and ask that you please email us.

If you have been using Pandora, we will keep a record of your existing stations and bookmarked artists and songs, so that when we are able to launch in your country, they will be waiting for you.

We will be notifying listeners as licensing agreements are established in individual countries. If you would like to be notified by email when Pandora is available in your country, please enter your email address below. The pace of global licensing is hard to predict, but we have the ultimate goal of being able to offer our service everywhere.

We share your disappointment and greatly appreciate your understanding.

Sincerely,

Tim Westergren
Founder

In such a case, if you still want to access Pandora then you need to somehow disguise your IP address and pretend to be in the

United States. Using all the various techniques discussed earlier in this book, it is possible to pretend to be in some other country quite easily. I am going to use HotSpot Shield VPN service to change my IP address and pretend to be in the US:

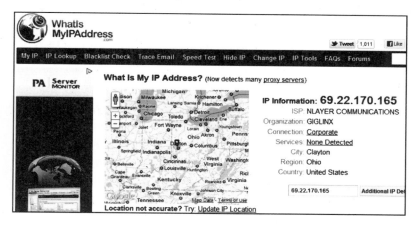

Now if you were to try to connect to the Pandora website then instead of getting the error message, you will be allowed to listen to your favourite music:

46   Remote Desktop

Remote desktop is a software or technology that allows a user to remotely access and control applications on some other system on the Internet. Just the way it is possible to use a remote control to control electronic devices at your home (like your television, air conditioner, music system and others), remote desktop software is like a remote control to some other system on the Internet. Remote desktop software usually work by transmitting images of the controlled computer to the controlling computer at period intervals of time. It is almost like a live video feed of the controlled computer being watched on the controlling computer. The controlling computer can also control the controlled computer using their mouse and keyboard. Typically, remote desktop tools are used by the technical helpdesk of a company or manufacturer to diagnose and fix technical issues on the controlled computer. Remote Desktop tools can also be used by users to access their home computer from your college or company remotely. Most importantly, they can also be used to bypass blocking mechanisms and access blocked websites and applications.

If you are working for a company or studying in a college, then chances are that they would have blocked access to all your favourite websites on the Internet (like Facebook, YouTube and others) and even blocked applications like instant messengers (like Google Talk, Skype and others). However, if you still want to access those blocked websites and applications from your office or college computer then Remote Desktop software can be very useful.

One of my favourite remote desktop tools is a software called TeamViewer, which is available as a free download at http://www.teamviewer.com. It allows you to remotely access your data and applications on a remote computer within a few seconds without any complicated installation procedure. If you want to use TeamViewer to unblock websites and applications on your office or college computer, then you have to follow the below steps:

STEP 1: Install the TeamViewer application on your home computer that has full unrestricted access to the Internet. Installation is very easy and does not require any complicated configuration at all. Once you have installed TeamViewer on your home computer, it will display an ID and Password which you need to note down safely. This ID and password will be required when you want to access your home computer from your office computer. Make sure you keep your computer switched on and connected to the Internet.

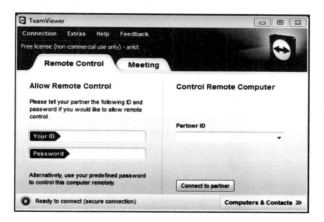

STEP 2: When you are at office or in college, if you want to access blocked websites or applications then you need to start your browser and connect to the website: https://login.teamviewer.com/ and log into your free account. (Please note that TeamViewer is free for non-commercial use.) In the Establish Quick Connection box, enter the User ID and Password that you had noted down from your home computer and click on the Connect button. TeamViewer will now establish a secure encrypted remote desktop connection between your office/college computer and home computer. Your system administrator will think that you are simply connecting to the normal business use website, but in reality you are using that website to connect to your home computer.

STEP 3: Within a few seconds, TeamViewer will establish a connection between your office/college and home computer. It will display whatever is getting displayed on your home computer on your office/college computer screen. You will also be able to access and control all applications on your home computer all remotely through the Internet. Now using this remote desktop TeamViewer secure connection with your home computer, you can unblock all the applications and websites that you want to access sitting at your office or college computer. For example, in the below screenshot, sitting in my office I am able to remote access my home computer and then use my home computer to connect to Facebook (even though Facebook is officially blocked on my office computer). As simple as that!

If applications like Google Talk, Skype and others are blocked on your office computer, you can still continue to access them using TeamViewer to access them on your home computer:

It is important to note that there are some restrictions that even TeamViewer has. If you were to make a Skype phone call using the free version of TeamViewer to connect to your home computer, then sitting on your office or college computer you will not be able to hear or speak anything. This is because TeamViewer only transmits recorded images of your home computer screen to your office computer and does not transmit voice in any direction. Similarly, if you were to play a YouTube video on your home computer's browser, then using TeamViewer you can remotely see the video, but you won't be able to hear any audio.

Some other popular free and paid remote desktop software are the following:

- Log Me In (https://www.logmein.com)

- Real VNC (http://www.realvnc.com/)

- Tight VNC (http://www.tightvnc.com/)

- Ultra VNC (http://www.uvnc.com/)

- Windows Remote Desktop Connection (http://www.microsoft.com)

The Tails Operating System

In this book we have discussed a variety of different ways of protecting your privacy, hiding your identity, remaining anonymous and bypassing restrictions on the Internet. However, if you really concerned about your privacy and anonymity on the Internet, then you will really like the Tails operating system.

The Tails operating system (http://tails.boum.org) is available as a free download on the Internet and has been specifically designed keeping security in mind. It is an OS that can run from a bootable live CD or pen drive and gives a user absolute anonymity on the Internet. Not only does it protect your privacy on the Internet, it can also be used to bypass restrictions that may have been implemented by your local system administrator. Tails uses *Tor* to provide users with secure encrypted anonymous access to the Internet. It has various in-built encryption capabilities which allow users to use encryption to store files, send instant messages, do email and browse the Internet. It is possible to install Tails OS on a bootable CD instead of a pen drive, but I personally prefer using Tails from a pen drive. The procedure of installing Tails on a pen drive in such a manner that the pen drive is bootable is slightly complicated for newbies and is described in detail below:

STEP 1: The first step is to obviously download the Tails operating system from its website. Please note that it is approximately a 580 MB download and will take some time to download if you do not have a fast Internet connection. You also need to download a special tool called Universal USB Installer (http://www.pendrivelinux.com/downloads/Universal-USB-Installer/Universal-USB-Installer.exe) which will allow you to install Tails on the UBS pen drive and make it bootable. Finally, you also need a USB pen drive with at least 2 GB of free space.

Make sure you have no important data on the pen drive since all or some of it may get deleted during installation.

STEP 2: Plug in your USB pen drive to your computer and start the Universal USB Installer software and follow the instructions on the screen. At some point, it will ask you to choose the Linux distribution you wish to install (we select Tails), choose the path name where you downloaded the Tails ISO image and select the drive on which you wish to install the Tails operating system. The complete installation process will take not more than a few minutes.

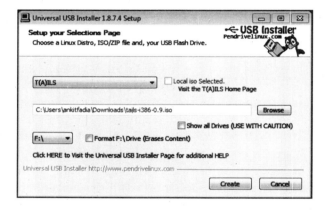

It is important to pay special attention to the warning message (that will get displayed on the screen) about losing all the data on the pen drive that you want to install the Tails OS on.

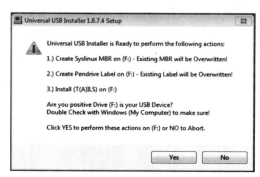

STEP 3: Once installation gets over, keep the USB pen drive plugged into your computer and restart your computer. Before Windows starts booting, quickly press F8, F11, F1, Esc or any other relevant key that you need to press to enter the BIOS settings page. Look for something known as Boot Sequence or Boot Priority and make sure that the priority to boot from the USB device is higher than the priority to boot from hard drive. The idea is to make sure that instead of the computer booting from the hard drive (i.e. Windows), it boots from the pen drive (i.e. Tails). Save the settings and restart your computer.

```
x Boot Priority
1st Boot Priority                          [USB Storage Device]
2nd Boot Priority                          [Diskette Drive]
3rd Boot Priority                          [Hard Drive]
4th Boot Priority                          [CD/DVD/CD-RW Drive]
5th Boot Priority                          [eSATA]
6th Boot Priority                          [Network]
```

STEP 4: The Tails OS should start automatically on your computer. The best part is that since Windows has not booted, all the application restrictions that existed on Windows will no longer be there. You are free to use whatever application you want, however you want and whenever you want.

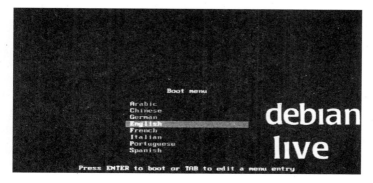

Tails OS is so popular because of the fact that it comes with various useful application preinstalled (like Pidgin Instant Messenger, Browser, I2P, Tor and others) which are preconfigured to give you anonymity on the Internet. Not only will you be able to unblock applications, you will also be able to use those applications to unblocked blocked stuff on the Internet. So along with application restrictions, any website restrictions are also removed using Tails.

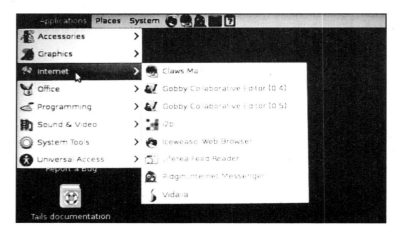

Firewall Tunnelling using SSH & Putty

SSH (Secure Shell) is a protocol that allows two devices to exchange data with each other securely in an encrypted format, hence protecting the data being transmitted. It usually uses the Port 22 for all communication. For example, if you were to connect to a remote server, then there is no guarantee that your username and password would be transmitted in secure encrypted format. This is where SSH comes in. It protects your sensitive information like username and password by encrypting it and securely transmitting it on the Internet.

PuTTY is a free, open source client that allows users to establish connection using SSH, Telnet and other network protocols with remote systems. It can be downloaded free for cost from http://www.putty.org/. Putty is also available as a portable application that you can run from your USB pen drive. The portable version can be downloaded for free from http://www.portableapps.com.

Let us assume that you are connected to the Internet and are behind the firewall of your college or company that doesn't allow you to make outgoing connections to remote Port 80 (HTTP or websites) of a particular website, say Facebook. However, you really want to connect to Facebook. What do you need to do? Just because the firewall has blocked access to remote Port 22, it does not mean that it would have also blocked outgoing connection to remote Port 22 (SSH). This means that you may be able to use Putty to create a SSH tunnel connection tunnelling through the firewall (outgoing remote port 22) to a remote SSH server that you have access to and then use that remote SSH server to connect to the blocked remote systems. In other words, your firewall thinks that you are connecting to Port 22 of a harmless system, but in reality you are using that system to connect to Facebook. There are numerous steps involved in firewall tunnelling using SSH and Putty:

STEP 1: You need to either set up your own SSH server with unblocked Internet access or register an account on a SSH server that has unblocked access to the Internet. This SSH server can be in any part of the world.

STEP 2: Use Putty to create an encrypted SSH connection to the remote SSH server. (Outgoing port 22, encrypted communication will be allowed by most local firewalls.) Putty opens a local port that you can now connect to in order to access the remote SSH server.

STEP 3: Once you have connected to the remote SSH server that has unblocked access to the Internet, you can then use it to access all your favourite blocked websites on the Internet.

Now that we know we know the broad steps that are involved in SSH tunnelling, let us get down to the specifics. Let us assume that your firewall has blocked outgoing connections to remote port 25 and 80 and you want to use Putty and SSH to bypass this blocking mechanism and access the remote systems.

STEP 1: Download Putty and click on Session. In the Hostname field enter the IP address of the SSH server that you want to connect to. In the Port field enter 22.

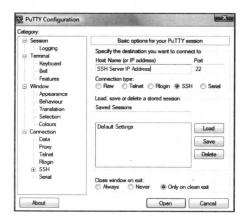

STEP 2: Click on Connection > SSH > Tunnels and enter the IP addresses and port numbers of the blocked remote systems you wish to tunnel to. For example, I entered 110 in the source port field & 192.168.0.11:110 in the Destination field then clicked on Add. Repeat this for all blocked systems and ports you which to tunnel to.

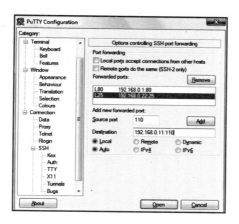

STEP 3: Based on this configuration, now the local port 80 on your system will connect to Port 80 on 192.168.0.1 (using SSH connection to SSH server) and the local port 25 will connect to Port 25 on 192.168.0.22 (using SSH connection to SSH server) and so on. As simple as that.

STEP 4: Now click on the OPEN button, you will be prompted to enter the SSH server username and password. You would have received it when you created an account on the remote SSH server. Putty now starts to listen to Port 80 and Port 110 on the local system. Now in order to access the Port 80 on 192.168.0.1, you need to start your browser or any other tool and simply type local host: 80 or local host: 110 and press enter!

It is also possible to buy SSH Tunnel accounts on various websites like https://camolist.com/sshtunnel/ which is currently providing a SSH tunnel account to users at a subscription price of $5 (₹ 250) per month.

Unblocking Instant Messengers

If you are anything like me and love everything that is related to Google, then I am sure you spend a lot of time chatting with your friends using the Google Talk Instant messenger. According to its website, for Google Talk to function normally, it needs to be able to establish connections to the server talk.google.com on Port 5222 or on Port 443. This means that if an organization wants to block Google talk, then they just need to block DNS lookups to talk.google.com and/or block outgoing connections to remote Port 5222. This can easily be done using a firewall or filtering device. Let us assume that Google Talk has already been blocked using this technique, so now in this section we will now figure out a way to unblock Google Talk.

Normally, whenever you start Google Talk and have successfully logged into your account, then if you open MSDOS or the command line prompt and type the *netstat –n* command then you will always see an outgoing connection to Port 5222 on a remote Google Server (highlighted in bold below):

C:\Users\ankitfadia>netstat -n

Active Connections

Proto	Local Address	Foreign Address	State
TCP	115.246.197.184:10668	209.85.175.125:5222	ESTABLISHED
TCP	115.246.197.184:10713	74.125.236.117:443	ESTABLISHED
TCP	115.246.197.184:10933	74.125.236.102:443	ESTABLISHED
TCP	127.0.0.1:1028	127.0.0.1:5354	ESTABLISHED
TCP	127.0.0.1:1186	127.0.0.1:1187	ESTABLISHED
TCP	127.0.0.1:1187	127.0.0.1:1186	ESTABLISHED

Unfortunately, if your system administrator is monitoring the traffic on the network then he will soon realize that you are spending a lot of time on Google Talk and will end up blocking outgoing connections to remote Port 5222 and DNS queries to talk.google.com. Once he does that, you will no longer be able to use Google Talk. However, you still somehow want to find a way to continue using Google Talk. What should you do?

STEP 1: Run the Ultrasurf tool (discussed earlier in the book) on your machine or from a pen drive or SD Card memory card. It will start listening for connections on Local Port 9666.

STEP 2: Start Google Talk, click on SETTINGS >Connection and enable the USE THE FOLLOWING PROXY option and enter 127.0.0.1 in the host field and 9666 in the port field. This will configure Google Talk to first connect to Ultrasurf instead of directly trying to connect to the Google Talk server.

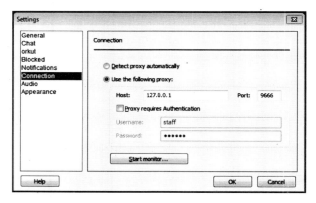

STEP 3: This simple change in settings will allow you to bypass the local network's firewall and continue to use Google Talk normally. Google Talk instead of making an outgoing connection to remote Port 5222 (which would have been detected and blocked by your administrator), in reality connects to Ultrasurf on Port 9666 on the local machine and then uses it to open a secure encrypted anonymous connection to the Google Talk server. If you were to type netstat –n now, you will notice that there are no longer any outgoing connections to remote Port 5222 and instead there is a connection to Port 9666 (Ultrasurf) on the local system that has been initiated by Google Talk. There is also an outgoing connection

to remote Port 443 (https port), which is the secure encrypted connection that Google Talk has created using Ultrasurf to connect to the Google Talk server.

C:\Users\ankitfadia>netstat -n

Active Connections

Proto	Local Address	Foreign Address	State
TCP	115.246.197.184:10944	65.49.14.74:443	ESTABLISHED
TCP	127.0.0.1:1028	127.0:0.1:5354	ESTABLISHED
TCP	127.0.0.1:1186	127.0.0.1:1187	ESTABLISHED
TCP	127.0.0.1:1187	127.0.0.1:1186	ESTABLISHED
TCP	127.0.0.1:5354	127.0.0.1:1028	ESTABLISHED
TCP	127.0.0.1:9666	127.0.0.1:10972	ESTABLISHED
TCP	127.0.0.1:9666	127.0.0.1:10978	ESTABLISHED
TCP	127.0.0.1:10972	127.0.0.1:9666	ESTABLISHED

Instead of using Ultrasurf to unblock Google Talk, it is also possible to configure Google Talk to connect to a proxy server from one of the proxy lists on the Internet. It is possible to find plenty of proxy servers through a quick search on proxy list websites like: http://www.samair.ru/proxy. For example, there is a Proxy Server 203.158.192.10 running on remote port 8080. We can configure Google Talk to connect to this proxy server in the same fashion as we had done earlier:

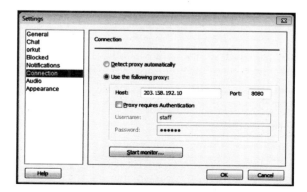

Now Google Talk is configured to connect to this proxy server instead of Ultrasurf and typing netstat –n tells us that there is no longer any outgoing connection to the Google Talk port 5222or to the Ultasurf Port 443. Instead all outgoing connections from Google Talk are now going through the Proxy server 203.158.192.10 on remote port 8080. At the same time, the local firewall is fooled and any blocks that may have been in place are bypassed. Many system administrators may block outgoing connections to Port 8080 to prevent the use of such proxy servers. In such a scenario, it is quite easy to find a proxy server that is running on other ports like Port 80. No system administrator will ever block outgoing connections to Port 80 since that will affect all HTTP traffic for all users on the network.

C:\Users\ankitfadia>netstat -n

Active Connections

Proto	Local Address	Foreign Address	State
TCP	115.246.197.16:6115	203.158.192.10:8080	TIME_WAIT
TCP	115.246.197.16:6117	203.158.192.10:8080	ESTABLISHED
TCP	115.246.197.16:6119	203.158.192.10:8080	ESTABLISHED
TCP	115.246.197.16:6123	203.158.192.10:8080	ESTABLISHED
TCP	127.0.0.1:1029	127.0.0.1:5354	ESTABLISHED
TCP	127.0.0.1:1032	127.0.0.1:27015	ESTABLISHED
TCP	127.0.0.1:5354	127.0.0.1:1029	ESTABLISHED
TCP	127.0.0.1:27015	127.0.0.1:1032	ESTABLISHED

It is also possible to unblock Instant Messengers like Google Talk, MSN Messenger and Yahoo Messenger with the help of secure HTTPS enabled VPN connections like Hotspot Shield that will route your connection through the VPN network, hence fooling the local administrator.

Web Messengers

A number of system administrators do not allow users to install Instant Messengers on the office or college system due to security, privacy and confidentiality reasons. If you are like me and cannot live without chatting with your friends even for a few hours, then a very good alternative is to use something known as web messengers. Almost all Instant Messengers have an online web interface that allows you to chat with your friends from within your browser itself without the need to download and install any instant messaging application on your machine. There are also third party web messaging tools available that are compatible with all popular instant messaging platforms. Some of the most popular websites that allow you to continue chatting with your friends using just your browser are:

Instant Messenger	Web Messenger Address
Google Talk	http://www.gmail.com http://www.google.com/talk/
MSN Messenger	http://webmessenger.live.com
Yahoo Messenger	http://messenger.yahoo.com/web
IMO (Supports MSN, Skype, Yahoo, Google, Facebook, AIM and many others)	https://imo.im/
eBuddy (Supports MSN, Yahoo, Google, AIM, ICQ, Facebook and others)	http://www.ebuddy.com/

In the below screenshot, I have used https://imo.im/ to chat with a friend on Skype even though installation of Skype is not allowed in my network. My system administrator gets fooled into believing that I am connecting to a normal unblocked website, but in reality I am using it to connect to the blocked Skype network.

Unblock Facebook Chat if www.Facebook.com is Blocked

Most colleges and companies nowadays are blocking access to www.facebook.com. This means not only can you not access the Facebook website, but you can't even chat with your friends using Facebook Chat. This is where very cool software called Chit Chat (http://www.chitchat.org.uk) comes into the picture. It is a free standalone Facebook chat software that allows you to chat with Facebook friends without the need of a browser and even if www.facebook.com has been blocked. Please note that you have to enter your vanity username from Facebook and your account password to log into Facebook chat using this software.

52

Unblocking Download
Limits with MAC Spoofing

Every computer has various network interfaces on it like Ethernet card, Wireless card and others that allow it to communicate with the other computers on the Internet. Each network interface on every computer on the Internet has a unique MAC address or Media Access Control address. MAC addresses are defined by the manufacturer of the computer at the time of manufacturing. Different network interfaces on the same computer will usually have a different unique MAC addresses. It is possible to view the MAC addresses of your own machine by going to the MS DOS prompt and typing the command getmac -V:

C:\Users\ankitfadia>getmac -V

Connection Name	Network Adapter	Physical Address	Transport Name
Wireless Networ	DW1520 Wireless	C4-46-19-4B-76-25	Media disconnected
Local Area Conn	Atheros AR8132	00-26-B9-CF-61-57	Media disconnected
Bluetooth Netwo	Bluetooth Devic	C4-46-19-F2-AF-D1	Media disconnected
Wireless Networ	Microsoft Virtu	C4-46-19-4B-76-25	Media disconnected

A number of companies, colleges and organizations have a policy on how much data each user can download from the Internet in a specific amount of time. This is usually done to manage bandwidth and resources on the network. Typically such download limits are enforced by recording the MAC address of all users on the network and then keeping track of the amount of data downloaded by all the MAC addresses. As soon as a particular MAC address reaches its respective download limit, then their Internet access is taken away.

Once you have reached the download limit assigned to your MAC address, if you want to still continue to download data from the Internet, then you can try to change your MAC address using a technique called MAC spoofing. If you change your MAC address to a new MAC address, then you may be able to fool your network into allowing you to continue to download stuff from the Internet. There is a very cool free utility called MacMakeUp that allows you to easily change your MAC address. Just select the adapter (the MAC address you want change), type a new MAC address and click on the CHANGE button. You may have to disconnect and reconnect to the network for the MAC spoofing to come into effect.

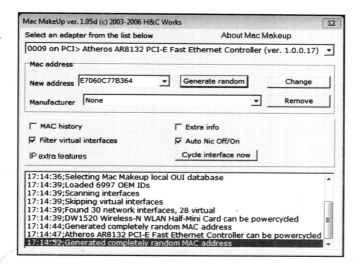

Some other tools that allow you to perform MAC spoofing are Mad Macs, Ether Change, Bwmachak and others. It is also possible to manually change your MAC address from the Windows registry.

If you want to bypass your download limit using MAC spoofing, then normally you will have to change your MAC address to that of some other valid user on the network. So the obvious question now is how you can find out somebody else's MAC address. It is quite easy to find out some other user's MAC address by simply running a data sniffer on your machine to sniff data packets being sent across the network. Once you change your MAC address and pretend to be some other user, then you will be able to continue downloading data as long as the user you are pretending to be does not reach their download limit. The firewall thinks that some other user is downloading data, but in reality it is you who is downloading data pretending to be somebody else! On some networks, administrators have no restriction on the amount of data an administrator's computer can download. This means that if you are able to spoof your MAC address and pretend to be the one of the administrators then you may be able to get unlimited downloads on your machine as well!

Unblocking Download Limits with Password Cracking

Some networks implement a download restriction on system based on their respective user accounts instead of MAC addresses. They will keep a track of amount of data each user account has downloaded and will block a particular user as soon as they have reached their download limit. In such a case, spoofing your MAC address will not allow you to bypass the download restriction. Instead you will have to crack the password of some other user on the network and then use their account to continue to download data from the Internet until even their limit is reached!

There is a very cool network password cracking tool called THC Hydra. It can be downloaded free of cost from http://thc.org/thc-hydra/. It is a parallelized login password cracker

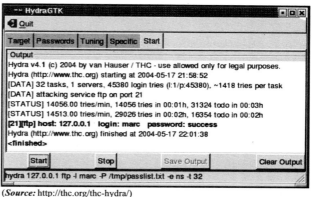

(*Source:* http://thc.org/thc-hydra/)

that supports various protocols like FTP, HTTP, POP, SQL, Oracle, Telnet and many others. THC Hydra can be used to crack the password of some other user on the network within anywhere between a few seconds to a few hours (depending upon how strong the password is). THC Hydra is known to be one of the fastest network password cracking tools available on the Internet. Once you have cracked some other user's account password then you can connect to the network pretending to be that user and continue to access the Internet even after your download limit has been reached. As simple as that!

Unblocking Access to USB Ports

Many system administrators block USB ports and do not allow users to use their personal USB pen drives on college or company computers. This can be quite annoying if you want to copy files back and forth or want to run applications from your pen drive. One of the most common techniques of blocking a pen drive is through the Windows registry by following the below steps:

STEP 1: Click on the Start Button Orb > RUN and type regedit to open the Windows Registry

STEP 2: Browse to the below registry hive:

HKEY_LOCAL_MACHINE\SYSTEM\CurrentControlSet\ Services\USBSTOR

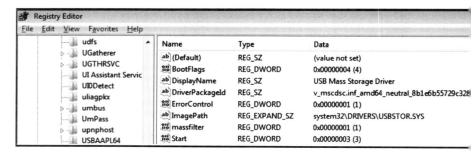

STEP 3: On the right hand pane, double click on the registry key START and change its value from 3 to 4. This will disable the USB port.

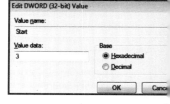

To enable a USB port that has been disabled using this technique, you need to simply change the value of the registry key START back to 3. As simple as that!

Unblocking Access to the USB Ports Part 2

Many system administrators block the USB ports using the BIOS settings instead of through the Windows registry. Usually blocking USB ports from the BIOS is much more effective than doing it through the Windows Registry. As soon as computer boots, even before Windows starts, you can enter the BIOS settings by pressing F8 or F12 or Esc (it varies from computer to computer). Once you open the BIOS, you will see something like the following displayed on the screen:

Select the ENTER SETUP option to enter BIOS settings page, which will look something like the following:

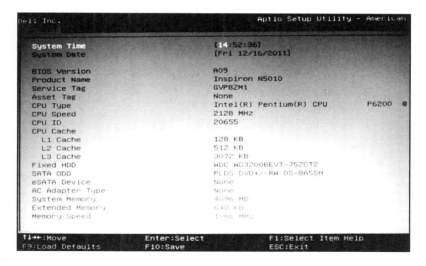

Select the Advanced Options and look for the *External USB Ports* option. Next to it there will be an option to DISABLE or ENABLE them:

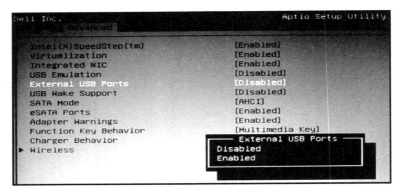

Finally, save the changes made to the BIOS settings page and restart the computer. The USB ports would now have been disabled (or enabled). As simple as that!

Sometimes it is not possible to change the BIOS settings since the system administrator may have put a password on the BIOS. In such a scenario the following techniques can be used to bypass or crack the BIOS password:

- All BIOS manufacturers have default passwords that may give you access irrespective of what the actual password is. You can have find default passwords for almost all types of BIOS software on the Internet.

- It is possible to reset the BIOS password by opening the computer case using a screw driver and removing the CMOS battery and putting it back in. This will reset the BIOS password since without the CMOS battery the computer cannot remember the various BIOS settings including the password. This is a lot tougher to do on a laptop than on a desktop.

Unblocking Applications

On most computers in organizations, colleges and companies, installing new applications is not allowed. Your network administrator would normally have taken away the rights that are required to install applications. You only need to manage with the existing applications or the ones that they give you the permission to use. This can obviously become quite stifling and frustrating after a while. This is where something known as portable applications are so useful.

Portable Applications are applications that can run independently on their own straight from a pen drive, memory card, camera, MP3 Player or CD without the need of an operating system or without the need of making any changes to the system files. Once portable applications are used on a computer they do not leave behind any temporary files, system file changes or registry changes on it. These qualities make portable applications very useful for people who want to run applications on a system that are not allowed. There are portable versions of almost all popular web applications like browsers, instant messengers, torrents and others.

Let us assume that your system administrator has uninstalled Google Talk or Skype from your system and has not given you the rights to install any new applications on your machine. You are really desperate to chat with your friends. What do you do? This is where portable applications come into the picture. Since portable applications do not require anything to be installed, neither do they require any changes to be made on the host machine, they are ideal in case of application restrictions. There is a very good freely downloadable portable instant messenger application called Pidgin (http://www.portableapps.com) that runs directly from a USB pen drive and allows you to connect to all the popular instant messenger accounts like Google Talk, MSN, Yahoo and others. The steps that you need to follow to use a portable application like Pidgin are:

STEP 1: Download Pidgin Portable from the Internet and install it on a USB pen drive of your choice. The complete application along with all the files it requires to run will get installed in a folder in your pen drive.

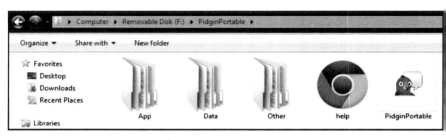

STEP 2: Plug the USB pen drive to the machine which has put in place restrictions to prevent you from using instant messengers. Browse to the folder where Pidgin has been installed on the pen drive and double click on the Pidgin Portable icon to launch the application. No installation will be required. It will allow you to connect to most popular Instant Messengers like Google Talk, Yahoo Messenger, Facebook and others. Type your respective user name and password and start chatting! Once you are done chatting, just exit the application and it will not leave any traces behind on your computer.

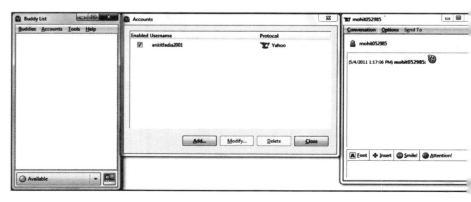

Similarly it is possible to run portable versions of a variety of different applications that are common not allowed to be installed by system administrators in colleges and companies. For example,

- Firefox Mozilla Portable can be used to browse without restrictions in case the browser installed on your computer has some website blocks in place.

- μTorrent Portable can be used to download torrents if installing torrent download clients on your computer is not allowed.

- Skype Portable can be used to chat and make phone calls using Skype even if installing Skype on your computer is not allowed.

- And many others.

57 Bootable Operating Systems

Many system administrators have a bad habit of putting a lot of restrictions on what applications can be installed on the computer and what can be done with them. In the previous section we have already seen how to use portable applications to bypass such restrictions. Another very useful workaround such application related restrictions is to simply switch to some other operating system like a bootable CD or USB pen drive Linux distribution like Ubuntu, Knoppix and others. Typically application restrictions that a system administrator may have put in place will become active only once the Windows operating system boots. This means that if Windows does not boot and some other operating system boots, then the application restrictions will not be active. In other words, if you are able to boot into some other operating system that is installed on your CD or USB pen drive then none of the Windows-based application restrictions will be applicable and you can use all applications of your choice. It is possible to install, boot and run Linux operating systems from CDs, DVDs, USB pen drives, MP3 players and even cameras!

Some of the most popular bootable Linux distributions and their respective websites are mentioned below:

Name of Linux Distribution	Website
Knoppix	http://www.knoppix.net
Ubuntu (my favourite!)	http://www.ubuntu.com
Fedora	http://fedoraproject.org
Slax	http://www.slax.org
Tails	http://tails.boum.org
Linux Mint	http://www.linuxmint.com

The various steps involved in downloading, creating and using a bootable Linux distribution are the following:

STEP 1: Download the LIVE CD or LIVE USB pen drive version of the Linux distribution of your choice that you want to use from their respective website.

STEP 2: Install the Linux distribution on a CD or DVD (using any disc burning tool like Nero, InfraRecorder or others). Make sure that you choose the bootable CD or LIVE CD option when you are running the disc burning tool. It is also possible to install the Linux distribution of your choice on a USB pen drive, MP3 player, camera and other USB based devices (using any USB installation tool like Universal USB Installer, CD2USB, LiveUSB Install and others). Creating the bootable CD, DVD or USB device is usually the trickiest step and most newbies are likely to make a mistake in this step. So be extra careful during this step.

STEP 3: Once you have created the bootable CD or USB device, restart your computer. Even before Windows boots, you need to enter the BIOS settings page by pressing F8, F11, ESC or the relevant applicable shortcut key. In the BIOS, you need to look for something known as the Boot Sequence or Boot Priority. Make sure that the boot sequence has the boot from USB or CD option at a higher boot priority than the boot from hard drive option. This will ensure that when you start your computer, instead of Windows starting, the Linux distribution of your choice will start. Once you boot into Linux, then you can freely use all applications of your choice without any restrictions. As simple as that!

It is useful to note that instead of booting into a Linux operating system, it is also possible to boot into a Windows or MAC operating system from a CD or Pen Drive.

Unblocking Torrents

Every organization pays a lot of money to buy bandwidth and since they are paying so much money for bandwidth, most organizations will do everything they possibly can to prevent its misuse. Peer to Peer (P2P) file sharing is probably one of the largest bandwidth eaters for most networks around the world, more so in colleges than companies. Hence, most networks tend to implement strong solutions to block P2P file sharing software. Besides being big bandwidth eaters, most of the content (like videos, songs and software) that is downloaded by users using P2P file sharing software is normally pirated and illegal. This is yet another thing that colleges and companies obviously don't like about P2P sharing tools. Moreover, a number of spyware and malware are known to spread through P2P networks. All these reasons put together make P2P networks one of the biggest enemies for system administrators. In this section, we will understand how most networks block P2P file sharing and how it may be possible for us to bypass those blocking mechanisms. Let us start by discussing some basic terminologies:

- **P2P File Sharing:** is the technique of connecting to a peer-to-peer network where you download files directly from the computers of other users on the network.

- **BitTorrent:** This is one of the most popular P2P file sharing protocols that is used to transfer large amounts of data on the Internet.

- **Torrent:** This is a file with a .torrent extension that contains metadata information about the location of some target file that needs to be downloaded by a user. It does not contain any information about the content of the file that needs to be downloaded. Without the torrent file, you cannot download any data from a P2P file sharing network.

- **µTorrent:** This is an open source client software that allows users to use the BitTorrent protocol to share files with other peers. It is one of the most popular torrent clients.

Most system administrators use any or all of the below techniques to block the use of BitTorrent on the network:

- Disable installation of torrent clients like µTorrents on your system. The assumption is that without a torrent client, a user will not be able to download a torrent file.

- Block the download of any file that has a .torrent file extension. All torrent meta files have a .torrent extension. If a user is not able to download the torrent metafile, then it will not know the location of the target file and hence will not be able to successfully download it.

- Blocking the ports used by torrent clients like µTorrent.

Let us now see how easy it is for users to bypass these commonly used blocking mechanisms.

If your administrator does not allow you to install torrent clients on your system, then it is still possible for you to download torrents with the help of web based torrent clients which allow you to download the torrent file from right within your browser! No need to install anything on your computer. One such web-based torrent download client is a website known as http://www.bitlet.org. Just start your browser, open this website and in the save provided type the URL of the torrent file you wish to download and you will be able to download the torrent from within your browser itself.

When there are restrictions on installing applications on your system another good alternative is to use portable versions of your favourite BitTorrent clients like µTorrent. The portable version of µTorrent can run directly from a USB pen drive without the need to install anything on the local system. As long as USB ports are enabled on your machine, you can continue to use the portable version of µTorrent to download all your favourite torrents.

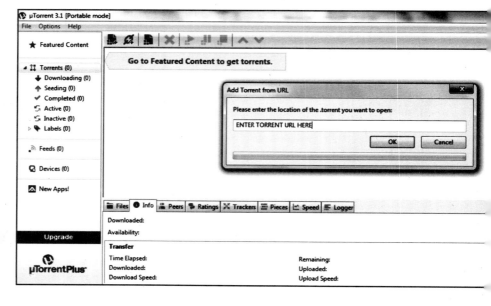

Now that you have managed to bypass the first commonly seen restriction that prevents you from installing a torrent client on your system, let us see how to get past the firewall restriction that blocks you from downloading files with a .torrent extension. There is a fantastic website called http://www.torrent2exe.com which allows you to download the torrent file directly from within the browser and at the same time changes the extension of the torrent file from .torrent to .exe. This means that your college or company network administrator will think that you are downloading a .exe executable file, but in reality you will be downloading .torrent file. Once you finish downloading the .exe file and execute it, it will automatically start downloading your torrent.

An even better website is http://txtor.dwerg.net/. This website changes the extension of the torrent file from .torrent to .txt, hence

giving the impression to your local administrator that you are downloading a harmless text file. Once you have downloaded the .txt file, simply change the extension to .torrent and open it in a portable version of μTorrent and you will be able to start downloading the torrent file. As simple as that!

Moreover, there are also numerous browser add-ons or extensions that allow users to search, download and manage torrent downloads from right within your browser without the need for any software installed on your computer. It is possible to download these browser add-ons or extensions from the below websites:

- **Mozilla Firefox:** https://addons.mozilla.org
- **Google Chrome:** https://chrome.google.com/webstore/category/extensions

A quick search on Mozilla Firefox Add-Ons official website reveals plenty of options available that make life easier for users to download and manage torrents:

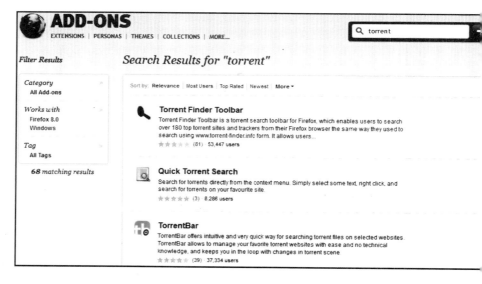

Unblocking Torrents using Proxy Servers

A number of companies, colleges and governments like to block torrent applications. It is possible to bypass such blocks by simply configuring the torrent client to connect to a proxy server. Let us assume that you are using the popular torrent client uTorrent to download your favourite movies, music and applications.

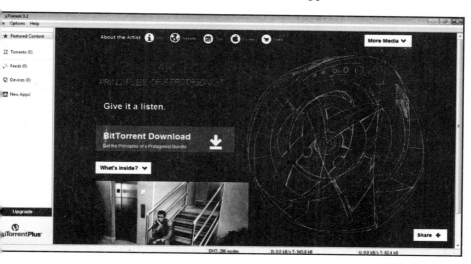

If you want to configure uTorrent to connect to a proxy server to bypass any blocking that may have been implemented, then simply click on OPTIONS > PREFERENCES > CONNECTION and then enter the Proxy Server details in the right hand side section.

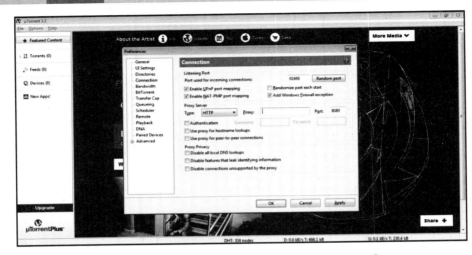

Now uTorrent is configured to connect to a proxy server and will continue to work even if any blocking has been implemented by your college, company or government.

Unblocking Torrents using SSH & Putty

Earlier, we have discussed how to perform firewall tunnelling using SSH & Putty to unblock access to websites. It is also possible to use SSH & Putty to unblock P2P file sharing software or torrents. The idea here is that you can use SSH & Putty to encrypt data being sent / received by your P2P file sharing tool, so that your local firewall or filtering device will allow the data to pass though. This data is sent in encrypted format to a remote SSH server which has unblocked Internet access. From there, the SSH server carries out unencrypted communication with the destination system, hence allowing you to use P2P tools even though they might be blocked by a local firewall or filtering device. You use Putty to establish an encrypted communication channel with the remote SSH server to avoid detection/filtering by local firewall. Finally, you need to configure your P2P file sharing tool (μTorrent) to connect to the local port that has been opened by Putty, hence completing the loop!

STEP 1: You have to either setup your own SSH server or register an account on a free online SSH server. Make sure that the SSH server has complete unblocked access to the Internet.

STEP 2: Configure Putty on your computer to connect to the remote SSH server and listen on a local port for connections. For example, Port 9999 or any other port of your choice.

STEP 3: Now configure your P2P File sharing tool to connect to the local Port 9999 and you will now be able to use your P2P file sharing tool. As simple as that!

Secondary Internet Access Mediums

If you are working for a company or studying in a college that has blocked access to everything that you love on the Internet, then more often than not all the techniques already discussed in this book will successfully allow you unblock access to an unrestricted free Internet. However, if nothing else works, then the best thing to do to get free unrestricted Internet access is to simply change the way you access the Internet by using a Secondary Internet Access Medium. The concept is very simple and straightforward. If you do not connect to the Internet using your college/company Internet access then you can completely bypass all blocks that their firewall, DNS server, proxy server or any other filtering device may have implemented.

USB dongles and data cards have become very affordable in India and 3G has increased the access speeds quite significantly as well. If you are tired of being censored and blocked every single day on the Internet, then maybe it is time to change the way you access the Internet. Just get a USB data card or dongle for yourself and start accessing the Internet using it to completely bypass any censorship or filtering your college or company may have implemented.

Most cities in India now also have public WiFi Internet access providers that allow users to access the Internet wirelessly either for free or by paying a subscription fee. It may not be such a bad idea to scan for available public wireless networks that are within range from your office or college. If you find a WiFi network that is within range than maybe you can ditch your college or company network completely and instead start using the public WiFi network to get unblocked and unrestricted Internet access on your office or college computer. This technique of scanning for available WiFi networks within range is called 'war driving'. It is obviously possible to scan for Wifi networks using Windows itself. Most of us already know how to do that. However, instead of using Windows, I would recommend using a specialized war driving tool. My favourite war driving tool is inSSIDer, which is available as a free download on the Internet and usually gives far better results than Windows (http://www.metageek.net/products/inssider)

C Address	SSID	RSSI	Channel	Vendor	Privacy	Max Rate	Network Type	First Seen
92:34:12:47:39	YOU Broadband"Help 9892577898	-68	11	Ruckus Wireless	None	54	Infrastructure	09:34:02
92:34:12:2C:89	YOU Broadband"Help 9892577898	-78	11	Ruckus Wireless	None	54	Infrastructure	09:34:02
67:06:32:A3:D9	tikona 18002090044	-4	12	Ruckus Wireless	None	54	Infrastructure	09:34:02
4F:AA:33:93:29	tikona 18002090044	-81	13	Ruckus Wireless	None	54	Infrastructure	09:34:02
92:34:12:33:69	YOU Broadband"Help 9892577898	-22	11	Ruckus Wireless	None	54	Infrastructure	09:34:02
92:34:12:2E:69	YOU Broadband"Help 9892577898	-66	1	Ruckus Wireless	None	54	Infrastructure	09:34:02
92:34:12:3C:69	YOU BB"RudeLounge	-79	1	Ruckus Wireless	None	54	Infrastructure	09:34:02
67:06:38:29:69	tikona 18002090044	-22	5	Ruckus Wireless	None	54	Infrastructure	09:34:02
18:25:00:57:10	TTML_W18F24_7	-71	6	Wavion LTD	RSNA-CCMP	54	Infrastructure	09:34:02
3A:99:4C:8C:91	ABMGYN-ATITHI		6	Cisco Systems	None	54	Infrastructure	09:34:02
92:34:12:3E:C9	YOU Broadband"Help 9892577898	-76	6	Ruckus Wireless	None	54	Infrastructure	09:34:02
18:25:00:57:11	Mgt_W18F24_7	-83	6	Wavion LTD	WEP	54	Infrastructure	09:34:02

Time Graph | 2.4 GHz Channels | 5 GHz Channels | Filters | GPS

How to Read Paid Newspapers and Magazine Articles for Free

Over the last many years, newspapers and magazines have spoilt us by not charging us to read any of their online articles on their website. Customers had to pay to buy the physical hardcopy of a newspaper or magazine, but online access to all articles on their website was available to all users absolutely free of cost. Things have changed in the last few years though. Most of popular newspapers and magazines globally (more so outside India than within India) like *The Wall Street Journal* (http://www.wsj.com), *New York Times* (http://www.nytimes.com), *Time Magazine* (http://www.time.com), *Financial Times* (http://www.ft.com) and others are no longer providing free access to articles on their website.

Instead they have put up something known pay walls. In other words, many of these websites have become subscription only where users need to pay a subscription to be able to read articles online. Some websites on the other hand, have adopted the *freemium model* where they allow a user to maybe read one article for free, after which they will ask you to buy a subscription. This can be really annoying, especially since for the last several years all of us have been super spoilt by being given free access to all newspaper and magazine articles online. Now obviously nobody wants to start paying for something that they are used to getting for free.

For example, I really like to read the *Wall Street Journal* regularly. Unfortunately, nowadays they have a policy wherein you are allowed to read only one article for free, after which if you try to read any more articles then you are shown an error message *TO CONTINUE READING SUBSCRIBE.*

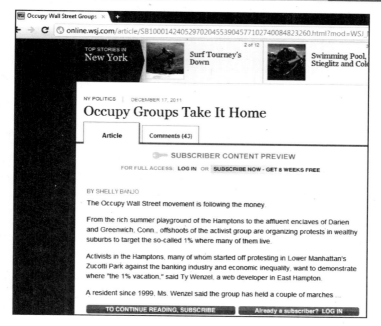

At this point, one option available to you is to take out your credit card and subscribe to the *Wall Street Journal*. However, many of us do not like to pay for things. This is where a simple Google trick comes into the picture.

STEP 1: Whenever you come across an article in a newspaper or magazine website that is blocked or incompletely displayed and the website is asking you to subscribe to continue reading the article, then all you need to do as the first step is to simply copy the article headline or title. In this example, the article headline or title is *Occupy Groups Take It Home*.

STEP 2: Open the Google search engine and search for the keywords 'Occupy Groups Take It Home'. Clicking on the first link that will appear in the search results will on most occasions allow you to read the complete article for free without subscribing to any anything. You can read as many blocked articles as you want by repeating this simple Google trick. No subscription, no payment, no hassles!

Another simple Google trick that you can use to access blocked newspaper articles is to simply connect to http://news.google.com and use the *site* operator to display search results only from a specific web site:

site:wsj.com Occupy Groups Take It Home

Typing this in the search box on Google will return only those pages as results which are hosted on the website wsj.com and have the keywords 'Occupy Groups Take It Home'. Usually, clicking on any of the first few results will give you access to the blocked article you wish to read without having to subscribe to anything.

63 How to Unlock More Speed

In the last decade, processing power of computers has increased tremendously. Internet speeds have increased quite a lot has well especially with the advent of 3G and 4G broadband connections. However, all of us are still always constantly looking for ways to make our computers run faster. It is obvious that the faster the processer and more the RAM you buy, the faster your computer will run. However, on top of that there are some simple tips that can be implemented on your computer to unlock more speed on it.

Disk Cleanup

All Windows systems come with the Disk Cleanup tool preinstalled. It can be accessed via the quick search option in the Start menu. The Disk Cleanup tool will search your entire hard drive and tell you which files you can delete safely to free up some space on your hard drive. The more space you free up, the faster your computer will end up running. It is recommended that you run the Disk Cleanup tool every 15 days or so in order to keep tweaking your computer speed.

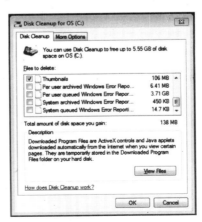

Disk Defragmenter

This is yet another tool that comes preinstalled with Windows. Over a period of time, sometimes data on your hard drive gets fragmented which makes your hard drive do extra work and hence slows down your computer. That is why it is important to run the Disk Defragmenter tool that will defragment data on your hard drive, making your computer run faster. Disk Defragmenter tool can be accessed through the Start Menu. Microsoft recommends that whenever your hard drive is fragmented more than 10%, it is a good idea to run the Disk Defragmenter tool.

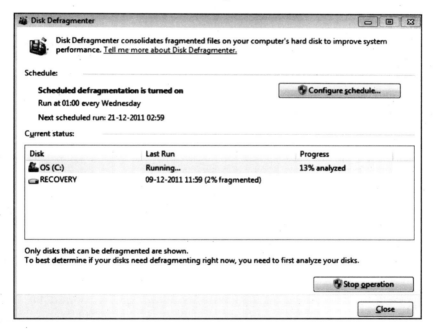

ReadyBoost

ReadyBoost is an option in windows that allows you to use the memory of a USB flash drive, SD card or any portable flash memory card as cache memory to boost your system performance. As soon as you plug in any pen drive or SD card to your computer, the AutoPlay options should show up on the screen in which there will be an option to *Speed up my System using Windows ReadyBoost*. Select this option and follow instructions on the screen to enable ReadyBoost. Now your computer will start using extra memory from your external drives to boost its speed and performance.

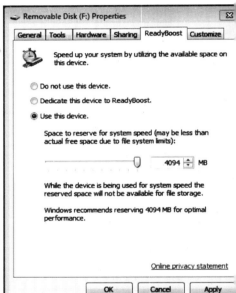

MSCONFIG

Whenever you start Windows, there are numerous applications that automatically get loaded into the memory occupying valuable system resources. It is important to run the MSCONFIG tool (accessible from the start menu) from time to time to check which applications are automatically starting with Windows. It is advisable to disable all non-crucial applications that you don't actually require or use, in order to free up some memory on your computer. This will significantly improve not only the general speed of your computer but also the amount of time it takes for your computer to boot.

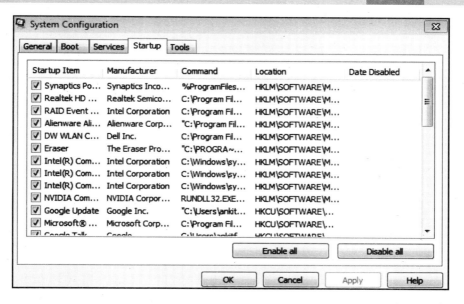

Disable Search Indexing

The latest versions of Windows use something known as Search Indexing to index your entire hard drive and help you search better and faster. However, Search Indexing has an adverse effect on the performance of your computer and can slow down your computer. If you wish to disable Search Indexing on your computer, then simply go to My computer > Right Click on C: and select Properties > Under the General Tab there will be an option to disable search indexing.

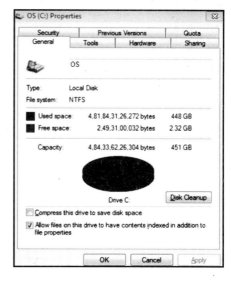

How to Block Ads and other Junk from Displaying in your Browser

Privoxy is a fantastic web filtering proxy that makes your Internet browsing experience much cleaner, safer and nicer and allows you to get rid of all the annoying banner ads and other junk that normally get displayed whenever you visit websites. Privoxy is available as a free download from http://www.privoxy.org

Once you have installed Privoxy, it is possible for you to completely customize its various settings and options based on your personal preferences. However, for most users, the default installation and configuration will be more than sufficient.

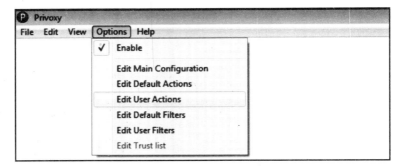

After Privoxy has been installed on your computer, you will need to configure your browser to connect to it. It is compatible with all popular proxy servers. The proxy address for Privoxy is obviously going to be 127.0.0.1 and the port number is going to be

8118. To configure your browser to use Privoxy, simply click on Tools > Settings and look for your Use Proxy Server option.

Now your browser is configured to connect to the Internet through the Privoxy filtering software. Now, if you were to connect to any website which normally displays banners ads, you will notice that the ads will be no longer appear! Let us open the website www.timesofindia.com and you will notice that all the banner ads have now automatically been filtered out from Privoxy and do not get displayed any longer!

According to their website, the way Privoxy manages to filter and block advertisements is actually quite simple. Usually, most websites serve ads on their webpages from specific commonly used directories (like /banners) or ad networks (like doubleclick.net) and Privoxy blocks all requests to such popular and commonly used ad serving mechanisms. Privoxy also looks at the source code of the webpages requested by users and replaces all references to banner images with dummy images. These strategies put together, ensure that most ads get detected by Privoxy and get filtered before the webpage reaches the user.

Not only can you configure your browser to connect to Privoxy, almost all Internet applications like Email Clients, Instant Messengers and others can be easily configured to connect to the Internet through the Privoxy filtering application. If for some reason, you find that Privoxy is not working or the banner ads are still getting displayed in your browser, then you can verify whether Privoxy has been correctly configured on your browser by pointing your browser to the special address http://p.p/. If Privoxy has been successfully installed and everything has been configured properly, then you should see a page like the following:

This is Privoxy 3.0.19 on ankitfadia-pc (127.0.0.1), port 8118, enabled

---

Privoxy Menu:

- View & change the current configuration
- View the source code version numbers
- View the request headers
- Look up which actions apply to a URL and why
- Documentation

Support and Service:

The Privoxy Team values your feedback. To provide you with the best support, we ask that you:

- use the Support Tracker if you need help.
- submit ads and configuration related problems with the actions files through the Actionsfile Feedback Tracker.
- submit bugs only through the Bug Tracker. Please make sure that the bug has not been submitted yet.
- submit feature requests only through the Feature Request Tracker.
- read the instructions in the User Manual to make sure your request contains all the information we need.

If you want to support the Privoxy Team, please have a look at the FAQ to learn how to participate or to donate.

Using this page it is possible for you to configure and customize the various filters, rules and settings of Privoxy. For example, you can control which websites you want to accept cookies from and what information you wish to reveal about yourself and your browser to the various websites that you are visiting. It is important to note that using Privoxy does not hide your IP address. However, it is quite easy to configure Privoxy to work with tor, hence not only protecting you from banner ads but also ensuring that your identity is not revealed on the Internet.

Unblocking Video Streaming Websites

A lot of system administrators in order to conserve bandwidth and resources on their network have a tendency to block video streaming on the Internet to prevent users from watching online streaming videos. A quick workaround such a block is to simply download the entire video instead of streaming it. There are numerous popular video download websites on the Internet like http://www.keepvid.com, http://www.savevid.com, http://www.zamzar.com and many others. The steps that you need to follow to download a video from any website on the Internet are the following:

STEP 1: Start your browser and connect to any popular video download website like http://www.savevid.com and in the space provided enter the URL of the video that you wish to download and press the download button.

STEP 2: Within a few·seconds you will be given the option to download the requested video in a variety of different formats like FLV, MP4 and others. Select any format of your choice and the

download will begin. Most popular video streaming websites like YouTube, MetaCafe, Facebook, Veoh, Megavideo and others are supported by the popular video download websites.

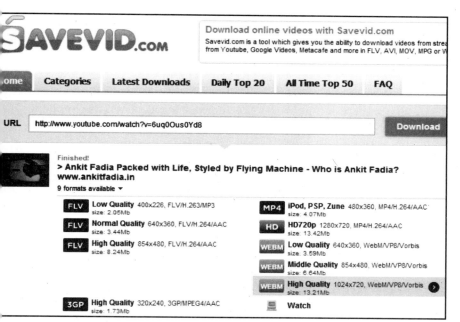

Most of the popular video download websites also have browser add-ons and extensions that you can install within your browser, which will make it very easy for you to download videos within a single click of the mouse button.

How to Download Videos to your Mobile Phone

In the previous section, we learnt how easy it is to download videos from websites instead of streaming them using video download websites like KeepVid, SaveVid and others. However, if you are like me and often access the Internet using your mobile phone, then you will realize that many of these video download websites do not work on mobile devices, since they require JAVA plugin support. In such cases, if you still want to download your favourite video clips to your mobile phone instead of streaming them, then all you need to do is the following:

STEP 1: Start your browser and connect to this cool website http://www.youtubeinmp4.com, which allows users to download video clips from streaming websites, without the need for JAVA plugin support. In other words, even if you are using a mobile phone you will be able to download videos using this website.

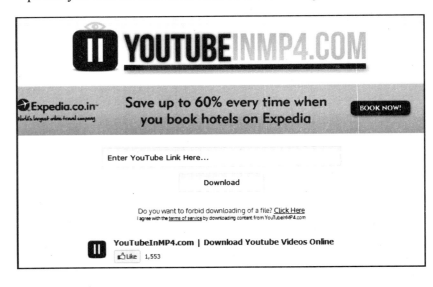

STEP 2: In the space provided, type the URL of the video that you wish to download to your mobile phone and click on the DOWNLOAD button. Within a few seconds, the website will display options of whether you wish to download the file in MP3 or MP4 format. As simple as that! I tried this on a Blackberry device and an Android phone, and in both cases it worked very smoothly.

HACKED – Ankit Fadia
Lecture Series

Ankit Fadia is a popular award winning speaker on various topics related to Cyber Security, Cyber Crime and Ethical Hacking.

To catch a criminal, even YOU need to start thinking like one. Unfortunately, most Internet users are clueless about the potential risks caused by computer criminals and cyber terrorism. With the correct mix of technical explanations and real-life case studies, Ankit Fadia in his talks provides participants with useful knowledge that they can apply to their lives on a daily basis and become more secure. Plenty of real-life case studies, a hands-on approach, best security practices and LIVE HACKING demonstrations will be used to unravel the fascinating world of computer hacking! Watch ANKIT FADIA hack into just about everything LIVE in front of your eyes!

Moreover, Ankit Fadia's journey from a 10-year-old boy who was gifted a computer by his parents to a 26 year old youth icon, author of 14 books, TV show host and consultant to various governments is awe-inspiring, astonishing and highly motivational to people from all walks of life. Ankit Fadia is a living example of how it is possible to make your dreams come true no matter how offbeat, different and unimaginable they might seem. His story will inspire people to think out of the box and pursue their dreams with tenacity, fearlessness and determination no matter what challenges come their way. Using examples from his own life, he throws light on how he managed to follow his dream, his passion and his goals in life to turn his hobby into a full time profession.Prepare to be SHOCKED, ENTERTAINED, EDUCATED and INSPIRED all at the same time. All his sessions are customized based on the audience requirements.

Ankit Fadia has delivered more than a thousand different seminars and workshops in 25 different countries to an audience of corporates, government bodies, technical specialists, police officers and college students. Some of the clients who have already benefitted from his sessions include Google, Citibank, Shell, Volvo, Wipro, Infosys, IBM, IDFC Bank, PWC, Cognizant, SAP Labs, Adobe, DIABOS, YPO, EO, FICCI, CII, National Police Academy, Indian Institute of Technology (almost all campuses), National Institute of Technology, Singapore Management University and many others.

To get more information about Ankit Fadia seminars, workshops and talks, send an email to neeta@ankitfadia.in or neetaagarwal4@gmail.com or call at 09820336782 with the proposed event, date, organization, city and other details.

Testimonials

"...Ankit's session was quite different from the other IT sessions that we have had at IDFC. His presentation style was COOL and it kept the audience captivated till the end. Overall, his session at IDFC was a BIG HIT..."

VC Kumanan,
Senior Director–IT,
IDFC Bank

"...We are immensely grateful to you for sparing your valuable time to visit the academy on Feb 11, 2011 to interact with the participants of 5-day advance course on computer & Internet crimes and ethical hacking. All the participants of the course have benefited immensely from your presentation and graded it 4.97 out of 5..."

Vipul Kumar
IPS, Assistant Director,
Computers National Police Academy,
Hyderabad, India

"...It's amazing how Ankit manages to transform normally drab and panic-provoking subjects like hacking and security into something entertaining, engaging and immediately handy! Ankit is one of those rare experts in their fields who can stir awareness, pique ideas and stimulate action in a completely non-abstruse style..."

Srinivas R,
Executive Editor,
Cyber Media India Online (CIOL)

"Ankit Fadia has an excellent grasp over his subject. The interactive sessions with Mr. Fadia also helped users to closely understand the various aspects of Ethical Hacking."

Subrata Niyogi,
Deputy Director General-Confederation of Indian Industry (CII)
Head, CII-Suresh Neotia Centre of Excellence for Leadership

"...The seminar was very informative and enjoyable. It was the introduction for many of us into the world of hacking. We were very inspired by the seminar and also very shocked to see several tricks of hacking..."

M. Raghavendra,
Indian Institute of Technology (IIT) Patna, India

"...That he is the smartest hacker around needs no reaffirmation. Ankit Fadia is a role model for all youngsters out there. Yes, his seminar was on HACKING but you get to learn a lot more from people of his stature. He being of my generation leads to an instant connect and hence the impact is so much more!! While he transports the audience almost effortlessly to a dreamland of HACKING, what the general public misses out on, is his love and dedication for his art, his professionalism with a personal touch, his down to earth nature and so many other finer details. Yes, you learn hacking while listening to him, but what you also get alongside, is an insight into the working of a genius. He is special..."

ArnabSen Gupta,
Manipal Institute of Technology, India

The Unblocking Contest

Have you developed your own tricks to unblock stuff online in your college, company or organization? Do you have your own ideas, techniques, methods, tools and scripts that are not covered in this book and that can be used to unblock stuff on the Internet? Do you have the latest techniques of unblocking stuff on the Internet that nobody else knows? Send them to me and if I like what I see, then I will publish your ideas along with your name and city in the next edition of this book (or you can choose to remain anonymous). Imagine, even YOU can get published and share your knowledge with the rest of the world.

The idea behind this initiative is to give a voice and platform to all ethical hackers in India to share their knowledge and to create India's largest collection of tools, techniques and methods of unblocking stuff on the Internet in the form of this book.

What are you waiting for? Get your ideas published by sending them to Ankit Fadia at fadia.ankit@gmail.com with the subject of the email as UNBLOCK. Make sure you describe your idea in as much detail as possible and also mention your full name and city in the email. If your submission is selected to be published, then it will get published in the next edition of this book and you will be informed through email.